MW01257701

The Lord Our Righteousness

or

Christ Is the Righteousness of a Sinner Before God

(The Old Perspective on Paul)

by

Obadiah Grew, D.D.
Late Minister of the Gospel at Coventry

"And be found in Him, not having mine own righteousness, which is of the law, but that which is through the faith of Christ, the righteousness which is of God by faith." Philippians 3:9

Edited by Dr. Don Kistler

Soli Deo Gloria Publications
. . . for instruction in righteousness . . .

Soli Deo Gloria Publications
A division of Soli Deo Gloria Ministries, Inc.
P.O. Box 451, Morgan PA 15064
(412) 221-1901/FAX 221-1902
www.SDGbooks.com

*

The Lord Our Righteousness was printed in 1669 in London
as *The Lord Jesus Christ, The Lord Our Righteousness; or Christ,
the Righteousness of a Sinner before God*. This modern
reprint, in which spelling, grammar, and
formatting changes have been made,
is © 2005 by Soli Deo Gloria.
All rights reserved.
Printed in the USA.

*

ISBN 1-57358-165-8

*

Library of Congress Cataloging-in-Publication Data

Grew, Obadiah, 1607-1689.
   The Lord our righteousness, or, Christ is the righteousness of a
sinner before God : the old perspective on Paul / by Obadiah
Grew ; edited by Don Kistler.– 1st American ed.
      p. cm.
   ISBN 1-57358-165-8 (alk. paper)
   1. Righteousness–Early works to 1800. 2. Jesus Christ–Person and
offices–Early works to 1800. I. Title: Lord our righteousness. II.
Title: Christ is the righteousness of a sinner before God. III.
Kistler, Don. IV. Title.

BT763.G74 2004
232'.3–dc22

                                        2004021530

Contents

Life of the Author

Obadiah Grew was born November 1, 1607 and baptized at Mancetter, Atherstone, Warwickshire on November 22. He was the third son of Francis Grew and Elizabeth Denison. Obadiah was educated first by his uncle, and then later at Balliol College, Oxford, where he earned his Bachelor of Arts degree on February 12, 1629, and his Master of Arts degree on July 5, 1632. The same year he graduated he became master of the grammar school in his home town and entered the ministry three years later. He married Ellen Vicars on December 25, 1637, the daughter of William Sampson. Ellen and Obadiah had two children: Mary, who was born in 1638 (and later married the nonconformist John Willes), and Nehemiah Grew, the famous botanist who wrote *The Anatomy of Plants* (1682).

In 1642 Grew moved to the parliamentarian stronghold of Coventry and preached to the troops there with Richard Vines. The city, which held regular fasts, was known for its godliness and sheltering of ministers fleeing the royalist army. Throughout the next decade, Grew established himself as a pious and orthodox minister, even debating such Baptist leaders as Hanserd Knollys, John Bryan, and Benjamin Cox. In 1651 Grew earned the Bachelor of Divinity and Doctor of Divinity degrees from Oxford. Three years later he was elected as an assistant in the ejection of scandalous ministers.

According to the non-conformist scholar Edmund Calamy, Grew protested directly to Oliver Cromwell against the execution of Charles I in 1649 and had gained satisfactory assurance, but was later disappointed in the outcome. Grew refused to conform to the Act of Uniformity in 1662, and so left his pulpit sometime in September. His bishop, John Hackett, allowed him to preach a month beyond the August 24 date, an attempt, presumably, to make him conform.

Grew remained in Coventry and preached freely in 1665, when the plague had so vacated the land that scarcely any "qualified" preachers could be found. In 1682 Grew, who had nearly lost his eyesight, was convicted of breaching the Five Mile Act and was imprisoned for six months in a Coventry prison. While there, Grew dictated several sermons to an assistant; so many copies were made available that conventicles were held. Nearly two hundred people were arrested for attending those meetings where Grew's sermons were read aloud.

When James II declared the Declaration of Indulgence in 1687, Grew returned to his congregation, who had obtained a building in West Orchard. Here Grew ministered until September 1689 when his health steadily failed. He died on October 22, and was buried in the chancel of St. Michael's.

Grew published three works: *A Farewell Sermon* (1663); *A Sinner's Justification* (1670); and *Meditations upon Our Saviour's Parable of the Prodigal* (1678). The second of these works, here reprinted as *The Lord Our Righteousness,* was never intended for the press, but was published upon the urging of friends. Its material is timeless because it clarifies matters concerning the righteousness of Christ and the justification of sinners. Grew was fully Reformed in his understanding of the church's doctrine of justification, and knew firsthand how theological inaccuracy was the church's plague. This treatise is especially useful for the new millennium, when so-called Reformed people want to parley with Rome and jumble faith with works (a feat which the Apostle Paul would most certainly shun!). That is not to say that works have no part for the Christian life; they certainly do. True faith is a working faith. But in the matter of how a sinner is justified before a righteous and holy God, there can be no question: "A man is not justified *for* faith, but *by* it" (Grew).

If you will but consult Grew on the doctrine of Christ's imputed righteousness, you will walk away with a better understanding of what Christ's death means for sinners; you will understand further why God sent His Son into a desolate world; you will begin to know how to live in gratitude of this glorious doctrine:

"Oh, let this doctrine of Christ's imputed righteousness feed us with admiration that the Lord should give His dear and only Son this name: 'The Lord our Righteousness!' " (Obadiah Grew)

Randall Pederson
Grand Rapids, MI
September 2004

To the Reader

I have for some years withstood the importunity of many for what I now yield to. The weight of the matter to other men's consciences, as well as my own, has prevailed over my loathness; and if your Christian charity may yield an excuse for what weakness is found in the manner of treaty, it is the favor I ask of you.

A sinner made righteous before God by the righteousness of Christ is, as renowned Luther used to say, *articulus stantis aut cadentis ecclesiae,* the crisis of a church standing or falling. For when the Galatians adulterated this doctrine, they were reputed by the apostle as removed to another gospel (Galatians 1:6). And on this point Luther himself pitched the field against the pope and the Roman Church, divers of whose grand advocates, though they strongly opposed this doctrine in their lives, yet owned it for the best divinity at their death, and some before. Bellarmine was not alone in his declaration: "It is the safest way to rest upon the mercy of God in Christ alone for salvation."

It may be thought by some that that statement of the preacher in Ecclesiastes 2:12: "What can the man do that cometh after the King? Even that which hath been already done," may be applied to this small treatise, after such large ones by so many learned men. And such indeed have been my own thoughts. Yet in regard, some of them are in a strange tongue to common Christians, others incorporated with other subjects, and many, of themselves, too large for every reader's purse and time. So with the idea that the more witnesses, the stronger the cause, yea, and that particular experiences in the point may add something to its evidence, as the widow's two mites did add to the rich treasury (Mark 12:42), I have let my pen go forward.

Now before I close, let me commend to your notice and practice three or four things.

In reading this and such gospel mysteries, you must believe above your natural reason, so that you give God the more honor (Romans 4:19–20). The object of Abraham's faith, which was accounted to him for righteousness (Genesis 15:6 and 18:12), was of that nature, whereas Sarah laughed, who therein was an image of natural reason.

In your reading and reasoning of this and such points of eternal importance, ever think that part the safest which least humors man's pride and most exalts the glory of God, since the scope of the gospel is to shut out boasting and bring in self-denial, which none can deny.

In all your thoughts and debates about this subject, seriously think to yourselves what is likely to be your opinion of it when you come to die. Bellarmine, as you heard, professed new divinity in it before his death.

If you have the opportunity to converse with wounded spirits and troubled consciences, with whom it is or has been as a specimen of the day of judgment, they will tell you whether any righteousness but Jesus Christ made of God unto them righteousness could serve their turn in the presence of God, or satisfy their consciences with a holding peace.

If you meet in this treatise with any mistakes in words, remember that you have this treasure in an earthen vessel, that the excellency of the power may be of God and not of man. And so you are commended to the good will of Him who dwelt in the bush by a servant of Jesus Christ, and of your faith in Him,

Obadiah Grew

1

The Doctrine Stated

"And this is His name whereby He shall be called, 'the Lord our Righteousness' " (Jeremiah 23:6)

The name "Jeremiah," when interpreted, means "he shall exalt the Lord." And indeed, in the text he highly exalts the free and rich grace of God in Christ to sinners. It is observable that, in his prophesies, Jeremiah mixes in frequent promises of the Jews' blessed state to come under the Messiah, as all, or most, of the other prophets do. And indeed, the firmament of the Old Testament is as thickly bespangled and beset with shining promises of the Messiah, and the blessed state of the church under His government, as the heavens are with glistering stars on a clear night.

These precious and glorious promises of Christ were the church's cordials in those times, in their troubles and fainting conditions. Thus we see that when the Lord would give King Ahaz and His people the Jews an encouraging sign of their safety, notwithstanding the fact that the kings of Israel and Syria were in a confederacy against them, this was the sign: "Therefore the Lord Himself shall give you a sign; behold, a virgin shall conceive, and bear a son, and shall call His name Emmanuel: God with us." This promise of Christ to come (though His coming was at a great distance) was sign enough to satisfy them in their present preservation; for herein He propounded to their view a greater salvation to come as a help to their faith in a lesser salvation now.

Truly, this may be a standing rule for God's people in all ages, to make promises of future great things to be cordials to keep the heart from fainting under present evils. So the assurance that Scripture gives us of Christ's coming again fully and eternally to save us should help our unbelief, and encourage our faith in His care of us in all our interim troubles.

In the text and context we have a famous promise of Christ, wherein the prophet hints at both His natures, and expresses one of His gracious and glorious titles or names, and therein His office between His Father and us. "Behold, the days come," says the Lord, "that I will raise unto David a righteous branch." Here He hints at Christ's human nature. He was to be the seed and Son of David, a branch of that stock. "And this is His name whereby He shall be called, 'Jehovah,' " which imports His divine nature, "Jehovah" being the proper name of God.

Then He expresses one of His gracious and glorious titles as to us: "Jehovah Tsidkenu, the Lord our Righteousness."

In Genesis 22:14 we read of Jehovah Jireh, "the Lord will see," or "provide." We read of Jehovah Ropheka, "the Lord healing thee"; of Jehovah Nissi, "the Lord my banner"; of Jehovah Shalom, "the Lord send peace"; and of Jehovah Shamma, "the Lord is there." In Isaiah 7:14 He is called Emmanuel, "God with us." And Isaiah 9:6 gives Him five high and mighty titles together: "And His name shall be called, Wonderful, Counselor, the Mighty God, the Everlasting Father, the Prince of Peace": and in our text, Jehovah Tsidkenu, "the Lord our righteousness." By all these we may see, and should see, how very much the Lord Jesus Christ is made unto us in His undertaking for us. As He "who of God is

made unto us wisdom, and righteousness, and sanctification, and redemption," Christ is made everything to
us that we should be to God.

Now whereas this name of Christ in the text is given
also to the church in this prophesy—"And this is the
name wherewith she shall be called, the Lord our
Righteousness" (Jeremiah 33:16)—it is no wonder that
the wife or spouse should be called by her husband's
name. And we find the church called Christ: "So also is
Christ" (1 Corinthians 12:12), or the church in union
with Christ.

I know expositors take great pains in sifting out the
meaning of this text, and do not settle on one. But we
may spare ourselves these pains if we think it not too
much to give the church of Christ this honor, to call
her by her Husband's name, "the Lord our Righteousness." And this is the name whereby she shall be called,
not from herself, but from Him who is made by God
righteousness unto her, and as she is made the
righteousness of God in Him. And so we find she is to
profess that she has her righteousness from Him, and
that she is to glory in it also. "Surely shall one say, 'In
the Lord I have righteousness, in the Lord shall all the
seed of Israel be justified, and shall glory.' "

Now the doctrine from the words, which will be subject of the ensuring discourse, is this:

**DOCTRINE: The Lord Jesus Christ is the Lord our
Righteousness.** The righteousness of a sinner is Christ
made righteousness to him. It is the righteousness of
Christ made his in God's accounting and his own; both
must be agreed on it. For if God does not account it so,
it is not so. "Who is made *of God* unto us righteousness."
And if we do not account it so, if we do not submit to
this way of being righteous before God, this righteousness is nothing to us. This was the doleful case of the
Jews: "Israel which followed after the law of righteous-

ness, hath not attained to the law of righteousness. Wherefore? Because they sought it not by faith in Christ," as St. Paul said, but, as it were, by the works of the law; they sought to be righteous in a legal, not a gospel way. St. Paul charged them with the same error: "For they, being ignorant of God's righteousness, and going about to establish their own righteousness, have not submitted themselves to the righteousness of God." And here was fulfilled that prophetic prayer, "And let them not come unto they righteousness" (Psalm 69:27).

And here we see sufficiently already that this righteousness of ours, that is, whereby we are righteous, or made righteous before God, is not legal, but evangelical. Man's first righteousness was legal, but that is not the case now. There is no such thing in being between God and us as legal righteousness; once there was, but now it is cast out in the bondwoman and her son. The law is not able to justify a sinner. Therefore the apostle said, "If there had been a law which could have given life," that is, justification unto life (as in Romans 5:18), "verily, righteousness should have been by the law. But the Scripture," that is, the law, "hath concluded all under sin that the promise by faith of Jesus Christ might be given to them that believe." It is true, Christ's righteousness, as in Himself, was legal, being the satisfaction of the law and justice of God in our behalf; but as this righteousness is imputed to us, so it is evangelical righteousness, because it is not righteousness in us, but righteousness accounted to us: "Abraham believed, and it was accounted to him for righteousness." So that there is now another way to justification, and so to life and glory, than once there was, which the epistle to the Hebrews calls "a new way." And this is the righteousness of Christ made ours, or Christ the Lord our righteousness.

Now in order to open and handle this great and

grand doctrine of the gospel, we are, as a preface, to consider what it was that made way for Christ to be made and called "the Lord our Righteousness," or for us to be made righteousness by Him. And it was this, the holy Apostle tells us, that made the way: Christ was made sin for us so that He might be made righteousness to us. "For He hath made Him to be sin for us who knew no sin, that we might be made thy righteousness of God in Him."

QUESTION. But if Christ knew no sin, that is, had no sin, how could He be made sin for us?

ANSWER. It is certain that He did not have the least taint of sin in Himself, and therefore challenged His malicious enemies in this case: "Which of you convinceth Me of sin?" (John 8:46). He defied the devil himself in this point also, as well as the Jews: "The prince of this world cometh, and hath nothing in Me," no sin to lay to My charge. The devil missed finding that sin in Job, hypocrisy, which he thought to have done. Aye, but he could find no sin at all in Christ, though reputedly he was "numbered with the transgressors," and by imputation was the greatest sinner in the world, since the Lord laid on Him the iniquities of us all.

So here is the answer to the question how Christ, who had no sin, could be made sin for us? He was so not by having any sin *in* Him, but by having all sin imputed *to* him. As Christ's righteousness by which we are made righteous is in Himself (it is not in us, but imputed to us), so our sins are in ourselves and not in Christ, but are imputed to Him and laid upon Him, as the errors of the offenders were laid upon sacrifices in the law. Thus the Apostle Peter speaks expressly, "Who His own self bore our sins in His own body on the tree." That is, He carried all our sins upon Him to His cross. He would not bear His cross, therefore they compelled

a man of Cyrene to carry it. It was a custom of the
Romans, as Plutarch observes, that the condemned person should bear that cross which soon would bear him.
Now though Christ could not bear His cross Himself,
nature was so spent in Him, yet He could bear all our
sins. The Lord would not ease Him of these, though
the Jews did of this cross: "The Lord hath laid on Him
the iniquities of us all."

QUESTION. But how did Christ bear our sins in His
own body? And how did the Lord lay the iniquities of us
all on Him?

ANSWER. There are three things to be considered
in sin: the pollution, the guilt, and the punishment.

1. The pollution and filth of sin. Christ did not
meddle with it. He could not meddle with sin this way,
so that in this way He knew no sin. He could not be an
idolater, an adulterer, a blasphemer, an unbeliever, or
whatever you call a sinner. Neither practically nor sem-
inally was He such, neither was He inclined to be such.
He was not, as the high priest under the law, a sinner as
well as other men, subject to the like passions as we are,
as St. James said Elijah was. The high priest himself in
the law was compassed with infirmities, and so offered
sacrifices for his own sins as well as the people's. But of
Christ, the writer of Hebrews said, "He was such a high
priest as was holy, harmless, undefiled, separate from
sinners."

2. As for the guilt of sin, there are two things to be
considered in it: the merit and desert of it, and the
obligation to receive punishment for it.

The former of these Christ did not take on Himself,
neither was He capable of taking the merit and desert
that is in sin. Christ, as for Himself, did not deserve the
punishment of sin which he suffered. Therefore Peter
said that when He suffered, it was "the just for the unjust."

But He did take the obligation to receive punishment for the sins of others; this He voluntarily took upon Him, and this was done with His own consent. And in this sense only was He made sin for us. He was willing to have our sins imputed to Him, to be transmitted from us to Him, so as to be obliged to bear the punishment of them, even that wrath and curse which otherwise we should have borne. The sinfulness of our natures, the sins of our lives, our sins past, present, and to come, the sins of all that have or do or shall do are imputed to Him when we believe in Him with a sufficient faith. Christ was willing to have all this sin imputed to Him, and put to His account to satisfy for, as Paul would have Onesimus's wrongs imputed to himself. And in this sense Christ was the greatest sinner that ever was by the imputation of God and in the reputation of men; for "He was numbered with the transgressors."

3. As for the punishment, though He was but a reputed sinner, yet He was a real sufferer for sin. He suffered penal hell, though not local hell; and the death He died for the sins of those who believe in Him was, in nature and proportion, the same which was due to us for our sins, and for the satisfaction of divine justice.

Yet we must distinguish between the essential and the substantial, between the circumstantial and the accidental parts of punishment for sin.

The essential or substantial punishment for sin to satisfy the justice of God lies in the punishment of sense and loss; and Christ suffered both of these. He suffered the punishment of sense, which made Him say, "My soul is exceeding sorrowful, even unto death." He suffered the punishment of loss, which made Him cry out, "My God, My God, why hast Thou forsaken Me?"

The circumstantial or accidental parts of the punishment of sin are these: total and final separation from God, which the apostle calls, "everlasting destruction from the presence of God," and total and final despair, "the worm that never dieth," the place of hell, and duration there forever. "The wicked shall be turned into hell," and, "These shall go into everlasting punishment."

Now these are, or are not, according to the disposition of the patients under the punishment for sin. In the imprisonment of debtors, imprisonment is of the essence of the punishment, but duration in prison is after the disposition of the debtor, according to his ability to pay, or to pay in time. He who is able to pay the debt may be quickly released; he who is not abides by it in prison. Such is the difference between Christ's suffering for sin and the damned's, as to duration under punishment. Christ was under the pains of hell as well as they; but He, being able to quickly pay the debt for which He was in, by reason of the transcendent and infinite worth of His person, therefore had quick release. But the damned are not able to make such speedy pay and satisfaction, therefore they abide forever under the wrath of God, "even till they have paid the uttermost farthing."

The same may be said of all accidental and circumstantial parts of punishment for sin: they are or are not necessary, according to the disposition of the patient's suffering. Christ was not capable of blaspheming, or of total and final desperation in His hell, as the damned are in theirs; nor was it needful that He should abide there forever, as they shall, being a person of such worth that He was able to make quick payment of the debt He took upon Him.

Now these things show us what great mystery there is in both the justice and the mercy of God: In the justice of God, that He would and could punish the Lord Jesus Christ for our sins; in the mercy of God, that He would transfer our sins and sufferings for sin to Christ, who could bear that which we could not, and could satisfy for that in a little time which we could not for all eternity. See also what great mystery there is in the love of Christ for us, in the sense we have mentioned, that He would bear all the substance of our hell.

Further, this should teach us to go to Christ in the terrors of our souls and consciences. He has had experience of hell, what is to be under the wrath of God and the curse of the law for all our sins; and He made a present escape out of the same. Surely, then, He is able to pull our consciences from under wrath as well as His own; as the apostle said of His being tempted: "For in that He Himself hath suffered, being tempted, He is able to succor them that are tempted" (Hebrews 2:18).

2

The Doctrine Opened

Now, having shown what was previously requisite to bring it about, that Christ should be "the Lord our Righteousness," that "He was made sin for us, that we might be made the righteousness of God in Him," I shall open the doctrine that the righteousness of a sinner is Christ made righteousness to him.

In handling this doctrine, two things must be opened and demonstrated: that Christ is our righteousness, and how the righteousness of Christ becomes ours so that we may comfortably so call it and use it.

The Lord Jesus Christ is the righteousness of a sinner, and that for which God reputes and accounts a sinner a righteous man. Our text is most clear for it: "this is His name whereby He shall be called, 'the Lord our Righteousness.' " Many other places of holy Scripture say the same: "And by Him [that is, by Christ], all that believe are justified from all things, from which they could not be justified by the law of Moses" (Acts 13:39). The reason of a man's justification is now fixed in Christ: "Christ is the end of the law for righteousness to every one that believeth" (Romans 10:4). The primary end of the law was to justify those who kept it. Now we ourselves cannot fulfill the law, and therefore the law cannot justify us. Romans 8:3: "What the law *could not do*, in that it was weak through the flesh," that is, through us or by our means. But now Christ does that which we could not do, that is, fulfill the law for us.

10

And He also does that which the law could not do, which was justify us. So by Christ, the righteousness of the law is fulfilled in us.

Of this there is further proof. "But of Him are ye in Christ Jesus, who is made unto us righteousness" (1 Corinthians 1:30). The end is "that we might be made the righteousness of God in Him" (2 Corinthians 5:21). And, "even so by the righteousness of One, the free gift came upon all men unto justification of life" (Romans 5:18). No man ever found any other way of justification but by the righteousness of One, of Christ, the second Adam. Christ is that fountain set open for sin and for uncleanness; Christ is that hyssop that David would be purged with; and Christ is the substance of all sacrifices in the Law, which were for expiation of mens' legal sins, and for their acceptance with God, as is excellently and strenuously proven in the Epistle to the Hebrews, in various places in that book.

OBJECTION. But the Scripture says, "It is God that justifieth; to declare, I say at this time, His righteousness, that He might be just, and the Justifier of him which believeth in Jesus" (Romans 3:26). So, "who shall lay any thing to the charge of God's elect? It is God that justifieth" (Romans 8:33).

ANSWER. This is true, but it is true withal that Christ finds the righteousness for which we are justified. The matter of a sinner's righteousness is in Him: God finds Christ, and Christ finds righteousness for a sinner. This is the case with debts and discharges from debts among men: though it is the creditor who frees the debtor, by acquitting him, yet it is the surety who discharges him by disbursing the money for him. So it is God who justifies a sinner, not imputing his sins to him; but it is Christ's righteousness that is laid down for the sinner and is, as it were, disbursed to God to gain his acquittance and discharge from guilt and damnation. Therefore the Scripture says, "There is no condemnation to them which are in Christ Jesus" Romans 8:1).

It is Christ who pays the debt. He lays down His own righteousness to satisfy it. As it is written, "Who was delivered for our offenses, and was raised again for our justification" (Romans 4:25). God acquits from no sin but upon Christ's discharging it, by both doing and suffering for us. He fulfilled all righteousness, and the Lord laid on Him the iniquities of us all, to make satisfaction and so reconciliation for iniquity.

QUESTION. But how then does God pardon sin freely and justify the sinner freely? Of this St. Paul speaks much; indeed it is a point that runs through the veins of the gospel.

ANSWER. It's certain that, notwithstanding that Christ paid our debts, yet God pardons freely and justifies us freely. You find them united in Romans 3:24: "Being justified freely by His grace, through the redemption that is in Christ Jesus." These two are not inconsistent, but are well agreed. For to us it's free pardon and free justification; we paid nothing for them. Isaiah 55:1: "Come, buy wine and milk without money and without price." We ourselves neither did nor suffered it, but Christ did both. The satisfaction that is given to God is by the surety, and not the principal.

This surety, and this satisfaction given by Him, are of God's finding and of His own procurement; and upon the matter, the money paid Him was His own, as if I should pay my debt to another man with his own money. And therefore this righteousness of Christ, by which we are justified and made righteous, is called the righteousness of God in Romans 3:21–22: "But now the righteousness of God without the law is manifested . . . even the righteousness of God that is by faith of Jesus Christ, unto all, and upon all them that believe." And

Romans 10:3: "For they being ignorant of God's righteousness, and going about to establish their own righteousness, have not submitted themselves unto the righteousness of God." And it is called both "the righteousness of God, and of our Savior Jesus Christ" in 2 Peter 1:1. So that though it is Christ's righteousness that justifies us, yet this is a righteousness of God's own finding and providing. He therefore, as it were, pays Himself with His own money.

Oh, the mystery that is in the pardon of sin, and justifying of the sinner! There is height, depth, length, and breadth in these things. There is as much mercy as justice, and as much wisdom and power as either. It is a depth admired and pored into not only by saints, but by angels. "Which things the angels desire to look into" (1 Peter 1:12). Ephesians 3:10: "To the intent that unto principalities and powers in heavenly places might be known by the church the manifold wisdom of God." It is a mystery admired in heaven as well as on earth (Revelation 5:11–13).

But for the further clearing of this doctrine, these things must be explained:

1. What necessity there is that a sinner should be made a righteous man.

2. That the righteousness of a sinner is not in nor of himself, but that it is in Christ.

3. What it is in Christ that makes a sinner righteous.

4. There cannot be any other way of making a man righteous but this, as the case stands now between God and him.

1. What necessity there is that a sinner should be made a righteous man.

The necessity lies in this, that God saves none but justified persons. "Whom He justified, them He also glorified" (Romans 8:30). "Know ye not that the unrigh-

teous shall not inherit the kingdom of God" (1 Corinthians 6:9). And because there are none righteous by
nature, no not one, therefore men must be righteous,
of grace and favor, before God can save them, if He fol-
lows His own rule, which most surely He must. "Whom
He justified, them He also glorified," and none else.

OBJECTION. But the apostle says that God justifies
the ungodly. "To him that worketh not, but believeth
on Him that justifieth the ungodly."

ANSWER. God does not justify them *for* their ungod-
liness, or *in* it, but *from* it. Though He finds no righteousness in them when He justifies them, yet He puts
righteousness upon them; neither does this way of justification leave any man ungodly, though it finds him
so. For what does the Scripture say? "Know ye not that
the unrighteous shall not inherit the kingdom of
God?" (1 Corinthians 6:9). And "there shall in no wise
enter into it [heaven] any thing that defileth" (Revelation 21:27). Heaven is called "heavenly Jerusalem" in
Hebrews 12:22 and "Jerusalem which is above" in
Galatians 4:26.

The ark may have clean and unclean creatures in it,
but not the temple; there were porters appointed to
keep out all who were unclean. So the church here is a
field which has corn and chaff together; but the
church in heaven has only corn, no chaff—not an ungodly person, not one hypocrite, all are made righteous
who are there, according to the apostle: "that being justified by His grace we should be made heirs according
to the hope of eternal life." Those in heaven are they
who "receive abundance of grace, and of the gift of
righteousness, which shall reign in life by one, Jesus
Christ." But this needs no further proof.

2. The righteousness that justifies a sinner is not in
nor of himself. It is neither in any gracious disposi-
tions in him, nor in any righteous acts done by him.

Where there is inherent sin, there cannot be inherent righteousness able to justify because it is evident that it is imperfect righteousness; and what good is in him, and what good is done by him, is now but in part, and that which is perfect has not yet come. That righteousness, then, for which a sinner is justified is a righteousness outside him; it is the righteousness of another, yet by grace and favor reputed and accounted his. So that it is by a foreign righteousness that a man is now justified, yet it is made his own when it justifies him. But how? Not by inhesion, as a personal righteousness, but by imputation, as a public righteousness, or the righteousness of a public person, another Adam; and so it serves to justify many, even as many as believe in this new Adam, or as many as believe in Jesus. For as Adam's unrighteousness brought many under condemnation, so the righteousness of Christ brings many under justification of life.

Therefore the question is how God makes a man righteous? It is not by putting inherent righteousness into him—for so men popishly confound justification and sanctification—but God does it by putting a sinner into a new state of righteousness, not of his own, but that of Christ's. And this point St. Paul understood well when he wished to "be found in Him, not having mine own righteousness, which is of the law, but that which is through the faith of Christ, the righteousness which is of God by faith."

Yet this must be granted and understood in this case, that as there was sin, and still is, imputed to men from Adam, so there is also sin propagated from him to us. We do not sin only by imitating Adam and our immediate parents, as the Pelagians hold, but we have sin from him by communication of nature. So it is between Christ and us: as we have an imputed righteousness from Him, for which God justifies us, so with this we have a derived and communicated righteousness which is within us by communication of the divine nature to us. That the children of the promise are made partakers of the divine nature is affirmed by Peter in 2 Peter 1:4. But this is our sanctification, not our justification; neither can it be because at present it is imperfect, and comes up to perfection and fullness by degrees, as the water of Ezekiel's sanctuary (47:3) which rose first to the ankles, then to the knees, then to the loins, and then to a full river.

But I shall more illustrate this point, that the righteousness which justifies a man is neither in nor of himself, by some particulars.

PARTICULAR ONE. The best works of nature cannot justify because they are not spiritually good. It is said, indeed, that "the Gentiles do by nature the things contained in the law" (Romans 2:14). They do many things which the law requires, and forbear many things that the law forbids. Cato was said to be a man very free from human vices. Moral virtues arise from the soil of nature. There have been eminent moralists among the heathen. Some parts of the earth bring forth not only weeds, but vines and mines; and so the nature of man may bring forth vices and virtues too. There are some sparkles, since Adam, of the law in the conscience of natural men about what is just and good. They have a natural divinity: and moral virtues are good, and very good in their kind; but not so good as to have any place in the reason of a man's justification before God.

Neither is this a disparagement to morality to say it cannot justify, any more than it is to brass to say it is not current coin and can pay no debts; for though it is not good for this, yet it is good in its kind. Moral virtues are lovely in their sphere. Our blessed Savior loved that young man for his ingenuousness. But justification is not the orb where moral virtues move; and therefore know that good works done by the light of nature or common grace, though good in their matter, may be very bad in their manner and ends.

So were the best of the heathens moral virtues, for they did not do their good works in faith or through faith in Christ, and so did not please God. They did not have this testimony in their actions, as Enoch had in his, that he pleased God. Whatever men do without faith in Christ, it is impossible that it should please God; Christ is the person in whom God is well-pleased, and with none else except upon His account.

Further, they did not refer the good they did to God's glory, but to their own. Christ told the Jews that they sought honor one of another; and the Scribes and Pharisees sought praise of men. What they did was merely theatrical to be seen of men. They were like the nightingale which, as Pliny says, sings longer and better when men stand by to see and hear. But when men's actions, that are eminently good materially, do not terminate in God as their supreme end, He does not value them. The Jews fasted in the fifth and seventh month for seventy years, and yet God asked, "Did ye at all fast unto Me, even unto Me?

Moreover, their consciences were not purged with the blood of Christ, and therefore they were defiled by blood, and therefore they were themselves defiled, and so all the things they did were defiled. Their works were but dead works because their consciences were not purged by blood. The Levitical law taught us this, wherein all things and persons were unclean that were not sprinkled with blood. Now dead works can no more justify a man before God than a will written with a dead man's hand can hold up in law.

PARTICULAR TWO. Men's repentings and sorrowing for sin do not make them righteous before God. Esau's tears did not wash off one spot of his profaneness; he was profane Esau for all his repenting tears. Oh, take heed of setting sorrow for sin in Christ's place; you may in this way cheat yourselves, as Laban did Jacob by substituting Leah for Rachel.

Sorrow and repentance for sin have a place in men's conversion, but none in their justification. Nor does that example of the publican break this rule, where Christ said, upon his penitent deportment in the sense of sin, "This man went away justified rather than the other" (Luke 18:14); for there is neither more nor less in the matter of justification. But our Savior used a popular kind of expression which only imports that the humble Publican's state was better than the proud Pharisee's. The Pharisee's postures were not taken with God as the Publican's were. If you put the Pharisee and the Publican into the balance together, the Publican was the more weighty in righteousness of the two; yet if the Publican had been put in the balance with the just and holy law of God, as Paul calls it, then it would have been said to him, as in the handwriting to Belshazzar, "Tekel, thou art weighed in the balances, and art found wanting" (Daniel 5:27).

Under the law, sorrow for sin did not serve the sinner's turn, though he was never so sorrowful for his offense. He also had to bring his offering, a sin offering, and lay his hand on it; and by that ceremony he laid his sin on it and so was cleared by transferring his sin from himself to the sacrifice for sin. Without the blood of that offering, which was a figure and type of Christ, his sin was not expiated. As Hebrews 9:22 says, without the shedding of blood there is no remission of sin. Indeed, sorrow for sin may help to bring a sinner to Christ's righteousness, but you must lay your hands on Christ your sacrifice; for there is your expiation of sin, and there is your righteousness.

PARTICULAR THREE. The inherent graces which

are in the regenerate do not acquit them of their sins and guilt before God, neither do their gracious works, nor their humblest prayers, nor their holiest lives. Abraham was not justified by any of his holy works before God, but by his faith: his faith in the promise, which promise (as all others) was in Christ. But what does the Scripture say? "Abraham believed God, and it was accounted unto him for righteousness" (Romans 4:3). And the apostle tells us that if Abraham had been, or could be, justified by the best works that ever he did (and he did many), then he had whereof to glory, even in his justification—but he could not glory before God. He might do so before man, as Job, David, and Paul lawfully did, being necessitated to it as they were. "Ye have compelled me to glory of myself" (2 Corinthians 12:11). But before God Abraham himself must say, as the godly among the Jews, "All our righteousnesses are as filthy rags" (Isaiah 64:6).

As for that justification of Abraham by works spoken of in James, it was the justification of his faith, not of his person. It was the scope of the apostle in that place and discourse to distinguish of faith, and to give the characteristic note of the faith that is saving. So it was Abraham's faith that was justified by works, but his person was justified by faith; for you see the Apostle Paul says that Abraham in his best works had nothing wherein to glory before God (Romans 4:2).

Yea, and if our best works were perfect they could only stand for themselves; they could not expiate the infirmities and evils that are in the rest of our works, which are imperfect. Abraham had his spots as well as beauty in his life. After he was called by God his faith was sometimes weak, though he is called "the father of all them that believe." Examples are when he went down into Egypt because of the famine and his dissembling with Abimelech. He drew Sarah also to sin at the

same time, even so as to endanger her chastity. Besides
that he had two wives, and whether that was a sin of
knowledge or sin of ignorance, yet it was a sin, as the
Prophet Malachi shows in Malachi 2:15: "Did not he
make one?" God could have made Adam more wives, yet
He made but one, upon which our Savior admirably
comments in Matthew 19:4–6.

Now if Abraham's good works had been perfect, yet
their perfection could not have expiated those that
were imperfect and evil. And upon all these premises it
must be concluded therefore that as Christ was made
sin by the Lord's laying our iniquities on Him, so we
are made righteous by God's laying His righteousness
upon us. This is in accordance with Ezekiel 16:14: "Thy
beauty was perfect through My comeliness put upon
thee, saith the Lord God."

PARTICULAR FOUR. Faith itself, as an inherent
quality, does not justify. A man is not justified because
of faith, but by it; not for it, as a cause of, but by it, as an
instrument in justification. Wherever faith is spoken of
in reference to justification, it is said we are justified *by*
faith or *through* faith, never *for* faith. Faith does not justify as it is a grace, but as it has an office which no
other grace has: to apprehend and apply that righteousness which justifies us. And therefore, whereas
Romans 4 says that "Abraham believed, and it was accounted to him for righteousness," you must understand it relatively, that is, in respect of the object of his
believing the promise of Christ; or else exclusively, as
that faith only is that in us which God makes use of in
our justification—not as meritorious of it, but as instrumental in it. And this also is to be understood not
of the habit of faith, but the act, as it acts on Christ.

Indeed, if faith itself were our righteousness, as
some mistakenly think, then we would be justified by
an imperfect righteousness; for faith is imperfect in us

as well as all other graces. We may often cry, and say with the father of that child with tears, "I believe; help Thou mine unbelief." Christ's own domestic disciples were but of little faith, and they prayed to Christ, "Lord, increase our faith." The apostle said, "The righteousness of God is revealed from faith to faith" (Romans 1:17). So that though we are justified by faith, we cannot be justified because of it.

3. The third point to be cleared is what this righteousness is that makes a sinner righteous before God, and for which God discharges a sinner from the guilt of sin and the damnation due to it. Certainly this must be some rare and admirable thing, a thing of infinite value and worth, which a poor sinner, yea a great sinner, may with boldness and confidence bring to God's bar and judgment seat, and there challenge God's sentence of death and damnation for his sins, and upon the account whereof the sinner can plead a discharge and release from a just and holy God. Listen to that high challenge of St. Paul: "Who shall lay anything to the charge of God's elect? It is God that justifieth. Who is he that condemneth? It is Christ that died" (not the sinner, but Christ for him), "yea, rather, that is risen again." And herein Paul shows forth a full discharge, and full satisfaction given, so that the law could demand no more, nor yet the justice of God.

And, truly, nothing but this satisfaction of Christ Himself could possibly have been of this value and efficacy. Adam's righteousness in innocence was swallowed up by his fall, so that henceforth it had no being. God does not so much as mention it (see Ezekiel 18:24). And the angels' righteousness will but serve their own turn. So that the righteousness that satisfies God for sinners must be a greater and a more excellent righteousness than that of the holy and elect angels. Therefore the author of Hebrews speaks of Christ's being made "so much better that the angels, as He hath by inheritance obtained a more excellent name than they." And because it is a more excellent name, therefore it is a more excellent office, which is to interpose and mediate between God and sinners.

Now this satisfaction which Christ gave to God for us, and which is by God imputed to us unto justification, because given for us, was His obedience. This obedience swallows up into victory our disobedience in Adam, and in our own persons. Romans 5:19: "For as by one man's disobedience many were made sinners, so by the obedience of one shall many be made righteous."

This satisfying obedience of Christ for us, and for our justification, was active and passive; it began in His life, but did not end till His death, for we are told that Christ became "obedient unto death." This distinction of Christ's active and passive obedience need not be quarreled with, though it is by some; for we must look unto Christ's sufferings not in abstract, merely as sufferings, but as suffering or passion in obedience. He became "obedient to *death*."

Now there are two things, say divines, in justification. First is the remission of sin; and this is from Christ's passive obedience. We have "remission of sins through His blood; and much more being now justified by His blood [that is, from our sins], we shall be saved from wrath through Him." The second thing is the imputation of righteousness; and this is from Christ's active obedience. He is called "the Lord our Righteousness," and we are called "the righteousness of God in Him." (2 Corinthians 5:21.)

Again, Christ's active obedience was necessary to qualify Him for His passive obedience, for had He not been holy and obedient in His life, then in His death He must have offered a sacrifice for His own sins as well as the peoples', which must not even be imagined. For the apostle makes this one of the great disparities between Christ and the high priests in the law, who were His shadows.

Another reason may be because Christ was to be our Sacrifice as well as our Priest. The sacrifice which was offered for sins under the law was to be clean and without blemish; so Christ, as our Sacrifice, as well as our Priest, was to be without blemish in His nature and in His life. So He was He who "knew no sin." He was to be "holy, harmless, undefiled, and separate from sinners." So His obedience in His life for us (which was His active obedience) had great influence on His death for us (which was His passive obedience). And so our righteousness, whereby we are both reputed and made righteous before God, results from both: from His obedience to the preceptive part of the law, which was His fulfilling the righteousness of the law, and to the vindictive part of the law, which was His bearing the curse of it.

This transcendent righteousness by which we become righteous (we who believe) thus, as it were, constituted of this double obedience of Christ, active and passive, is, for the infinite and eternal virtue of it, called "everlasting righteousness," and frequently "the righteousness of God," in the New Testament. It is called the righteousness of God, not as though it were Christ's essential righteousness as He is God, as some, though few, have thought. For that is incommunicable to us, and if that had been a righteousness convenient to our justification, Christ needed not to have been incarnate. The Holy Ghost calls it the righteousness of one man; and so it is called both the righteousness of God and of man because it is the righteousness of Christ our Mediator in both natures: God and man.

From this third point there flows these inferences:
- Absolution from sin (Romans 3:25) and exemp-

tion from condemnation (Romans 8:1) are not the whole righteousness of a sinner which Christ is made to him, or that he has by the righteousness of Christ reputed his, though some have had such thoughts. But doubtless all things pertaining to spiritual and eternal life come to us by the righteousness of Christ; therefore the apostle calls it "righteousness to life" in Romans 5:18, to live to God here, and with God hereafter. It is impossible that a man should be discharged of condemnation and not entitled to salvation, for Christ's righteousness leaves no man out of heaven whom He delivers out of hell. Whom He justifies, them He glorifies; and in Acts 26:18, remission of sins and an inheritance among those who are sanctified are joined together.

• Hence it most certainly appears that there is nothing of that infinite value and merit to interest in both a discharge from condemnation and a title to a new salvation but this righteousness of Christ imputed and passed over to us. For that inherent righteousness which He imparts to us, and which His Spirit works in us, cannot possibly do it.

That a regenerate man has inherent righteousness I confess; the Scripture calls such men righteous. "Thee have I seen righteous before Me in this generation," said God to Noah in Genesis 7:1. And in Psalm 14:5, "God is in the generation of the righteous." The Scripture calls these so in respect of their inherent righteousness.

It is not to be doubted but that this righteousness in the saints pleases God. It is said of Enoch that, in his walking with God, "he had this testimony, that he pleased God." Paul prayed that the Colossians "might walk worthy of the Lord to all pleasing." The word translated "worthy" does not mean "merit," but refers to decency. As used in Ephesians 4:1, "That ye walk *suitably* to the holy calling, to which the Lord hath called you," so the word is translated sometimes.

But this is a secondary pleasing of God. He is first well-pleased with us in Christ, as we are found in Him and His righteousness; and then He is pleased with the righteousness that is in us. The Lord first has respect to the person, and then to his works, as we see in Abel's case in Genesis 4. So that though the inherent righteousness of the saints pleases God, yet it does not justify them before God; this is done by a more perfect righteousness, not *in* us, but *upon* us. Indeed, as to the point of justification, our inherent righteousness must be denied and rejected as well as our sins. "All our righteousnesses are as filthy rags" (Isaiah 64:6), and this holy Paul knew well, when he sought to be found in Christ, not having his own righteousness.

The meat that Jacob provided for his father Isaac was good, and pleased him well; yet he did not get the blessing because of this, but by being found in his elder brother's garment. "He smelled the smell of his garment, and blessed him" (Genesis 27:27). So, though the precious graces, the holy duties, and the holy lives of believers and holy men are well-pleasing to God, yet it is not for these that God blesses them with forgiveness of sin, but because they are in their elder brother's garment, in the righteousness of Christ put upon them. "Thou wast perfect through My comeliness which I had put upon thee, saith the Lord God" (Ezekiel 16:14).

3

Guides to Lead Us to Justifying Righteousness

I shall add to what has been said in this first branch of doctrine some guides to lead you directly to that righteousness which must justify a sinner before God. Men are seekers in this point, but "few there be that find it." Israel sought it, but did not find it because they missed their way. "Israel, which followed after the law of righteousness, hath not attained to the law of righteousness." Why not? "Because they sought it not by faith," that is, in Christ, "but as it were by the works of the law" (Romans 9:31–32). The Philistines would not have found out Samson's riddle if they had not plowed with his heifer (Judges 14:18). And truly, as Elihu said to Job in Job 33:23, there must be an interpreter, "one of a thousand, to show man his uprightness." So doubtless it is the Spirit of Christ that must help a sinner to find out his justifying righteousness and show him where it is. So our blessed Savior says, "He will convince the world of righteousness" (John 16:8) as well as of sin; yet He does it by means. The Hebrews say that the Jews had hands set up in the way to point the offenders to the cities of refuge so that they might not miss it in their hasty flight from the revenger of blood. So to this famous city of refuge, these considerations, under the command and power of the Spirit of Christ, may be the poor guilty sinner's guides.

1. Consider what that is which God has assigned to be righteousness to a sinner; and this we shall find to

be the Lord Jesus Christ, "who is made of God unto us righteousness" (1 Corinthians 1:30). Nothing else has God's superscription on it for currant justifying righteousness in His eyes. Therefore men are much out of their way to the city of refuge when they think to find their righteousness in any good in them or done by them. A piece of silver uncoined may be good silver, but not current in pay because it is not the king's coin; so a man may have much good in him and done by him, and yet God will not take it for pay and satisfaction because it is not assigned by Him for that use—and this will guide us to the obedience of Christ, which has this assignment on it.

2. Consider what that righteousness is wherein God shows both His justice and mercy. Now wherein do these meet but in Christ's obedient life and death? Who ever fulfilled all righteousness but He? Who was ever made a curse for us but He? "I have trodden the winepress alone; and of the people there was none with Me" (Isaiah 63:3). The translation of our sins to and upon Christ was held out clearly in the sacrifices in the law, where by laying hands on the sacrifice's head the offender passed over his offense before he could be discharged—and this leads us to Christ for our justification, because our sins are translated from us to Him before we can be righteous.

3. Consider that all who are justified and made righteous before God are made so by one common righteousness—not every man by his own, but by a common stock of righteousness that lies in one public person. "As many were made sinners by the offense of one Adam, so many are made righteous by the obedience of another"—and this leads us unto Christ for righteousness.

4. Let a man work his thoughts upon the infinite justice and holiness in God, that He is a holy God, and

of purer eyes than to behold iniquity, but hates it; that
He is a consuming fire. And then let that man think
seriously and rationally, who it is who can bear the
hand of this infinite justice and the eye of this infinite
holiness; and there the sinner must find his righteousness. And certainly he will find no such person
but Christ, nor any such righteousness but His. He puts
no trust in His servants, nor in His saints. His angels
He charged with folly, and the heavens are not clean in
His sight (Job 4:18 and 15:15), the heavens where the
saints and angels are. So the saints and angels in
heaven cannot be the righteousness of a sinner; they
only have righteousness for themselves, and that is bor-
rowed too. As the moon receives its light from the sun,
so their righteousness is from Christ, confirming their
state there—and this still leads us to Christ for righteousness.

Application

USE 1. This informs us of what exceedingly great
weight this doctrine is; as it is a great mystery, so it is of
great importance. I may say of it, as Moses to Israel, of
the word of the Lord in his days, "It is not a vain thing,
for it is our life." There is no point of religion of
greater concern than the way of a sinner's justification
and standing righteous before God. David says, "In Thy
sight shall no man living be justified," that is, by the
law, as Paul expounds it. And so David, a man after
God's own heart, prays, "Lord, go not to law with me"
(Psalm 143:2). So the word may be read.

So this point of our being righteous by the righteousness of Christ is the vein of the gospel, and here
lies the vein of life. The law cannot give life. If the sinner had only the guilt of one sin upon him, the law

could not justify from this one sin. Aye, but the righteousness of Christ made ours justifies from all sin, sins from which the law of Moses could not justify us (Acts 13:39). Yea, and this righteousness is provided only for sinners (Romans 4:5). The angels do not have the use of it. Christ was not made sin for them, nor are they made the righteousness of God in Him, as we are.

Unless we try to mingle law and gospel, grace and works, and bring confusion into our state with God, we must keep up, and keep in view, this righteousness of Christ made ours, and that in both the doctrine and experience of it. The Jews ignorance, their willful ignorance, of this righteousness (for such theirs was), undid them, and damned many of them.

In the experience of this righteousness stands, first, the comfort of perplexed consciences. As is the righteousness we trust in, such is or will be our peace of conscience; when sin grates there, it is this righteousness of Christ made over to us that is the mother whose womb conceives and bears that true quiet of conscience that sinners have. Romans 5:1: "Being justified by faith we have peace with God, through our Lord Jesus Christ." Therefore Christ was first King of Righteousness (Hebrews 7:2) and then King of Peace.

Second, as this righteousness conduces to comfort our consciences, so also it very much exalts and glorifies God's free grace. As the apostle said in Ephesians 1:6, "to the praise of glory of His grace, wherein He hath made us accepted in the Beloved." It is by this doctrine that God had designed to hide pride from man, from the best and holiest of men, even from Abraham the friend of God and the father of many nations, even of us all who believe. Even he had nothing whereof to glory in before God. Yea, and Paul challenges all other men when he speaks of this righteousness in Romans 3:27 and 4:16: "Where is boasting then? It is excluded.

By what law? Of works? Nay, but by the law of faith,"
that is, "by faith that it might be by grace." We must cry,
"Grace! Grace!" to our righteousness of justification, or
for which we are justified. The Jews were to do this at
the laying of the headstone of the second temple.
(Zechariah 4:7).

Third, besides what has been said, this doctrine of
the righteousness of Christ made ours is the greatest
quickener of love and obedience to God as can be. We
are "alive to God through Jesus Christ" (Romans 6:11).
It is the second Adam who is a quickening Spirit.

Fourth, by this doctrine the whole or main fabric
and building of popery and popish anti-christianism
fall down. It was on this ground that Luther pitched the
field against the pope. A sinner made righteous by the
righteousness of Christ is, as that blessed servant of
God used to say, *Articulus stantis aut cadentis ecclesiae,* the
crisis of a church's standing or falling. It's the foundation point of the glorious gospel. When the Galatians
impured this doctrine, Paul told them that they were
removed to another gospel, and so to another Christ,
another faith, and another salvation.

So certainly a sweet state of peace in our consciences, the promotion of the free grace of God, a life
of godliness in the saints, and the death of the man of
sin, all hang upon this hinge: Christ the Lord, our
Righteousness.

USE 2. This doctrine may serve to exhort us to get a
greater acquaintance in it and to make a fuller use of it.
Oh, get into the clefts of the Rock, while God passes by
you with His holy and pure eyes! It is here that you may
behold God and hear His voice, without that fear of
Adam (Genesis 3:10, that terror of the children of Israel
(Deuteronomy 5:24), and that exceeding quaking in
Moses mentioned in Hebrews 12:21.

Oh, fly there for sanctuary when conscience complains in you and charges you with imperfections, yea, with filthiness in your own righteousness. And when Satan charges you with your filthy rags, as he did Joshua, the Jews' high priest (Zechariah 3:3); yea, when the holy law of God charges you, answer the law with this righteousness! Oh, fly into the bosom of this righteousness like a poor, hunted bird!

Remember that there is no righteousness that will serve a sinner's state but that of Christ. There is no such obedience as His in men or angels; nor is there any righteousness but His now communicable. Adam communicates sin to us, but not righteousness—Christ does.

It's true that God is pleased to take pleasure in His peoples' inherent graces; and so may they take pleasure in that there is such a thing in them as grace and inherent holiness, without which no one shall see the Lord. Aye, but if this should be offered to God as satisfaction for sin, He would refuse it and us too, and make us a terror to ourselves in the midst of all our own goodness. As Levi had father, mother, and children, and affections for them, yet Levi did not know them when in competition with God (Deuteronomy 33:9). So though the people of God have righteousness and holiness in them, yet they may not know it, neither will God, in the point of justification. Paul disclaimed his own righteousness. Therefore let us seriously give ourselves to the study, knowledge, and experience of this point, which is as much as our life, and that forever, "Christ the Lord, our Righteousness."

4

The Great Motive in Justification

We now come to the second point to be opened in the doctrine, how the righteousness of Christ becomes a sinner's righteousness. There are two things to be explained: The grand impulsive cause why this is so, and the way how this is done. This will require some particular branches.

The great motive to this way of justifying a sinner, and making him righteous by the righteousness of the Lord Jesus Christ, is the free grace and favor of God; it is an act of grace, and a famous one. The truth is, the Scripture not only holds forth that there is such a thing, but also acquaints us with the rise and reason of it, and leads us to the fountain and spring of this pleasant stream.

Surely, there is nothing that more endears us to God than the motive of our love and obedience, that is, when we love Him for Himself, and for what He is as well as for what He is to us; when we obey Him upon choice, as David did, "I have chosen the way of truth"; and when God Himself is our motive in our obedience to Him. So nothing more endears God to us than when we think of His motives in justifying us and saving us in such wonderful ways as He does; for these motives are His mere love, free grace, and good pleasure. It is said in Isaiah 63:9: "In His love, and in His pity he redeemed them." Deuteronomy 7:7–8: "The Lord loved you because he loved you," said Moses to Israel. And 1 John

3:1: "Behold what manner of love the Father hath bestowed upon us, that we should be called the sons of God."

We shall seldom read of God's choosing and justifying His people in holy Scripture without the rise and spring of those actions also being spoken of: His free grace and the good pleasure of His will. "Being justified freely by His grace" (Romans 3:24). "Having predestinated us according to the good pleasure of His will" (Ephesians 1:5). "But after the kindness and love of God our Savior appeared towards man" (Titus 3:4). Hence we see not only the hand of God open to bestow such rich privileges on us, but His bosom also opened, to show us that they come from that place, and there they have their reason. Doubtless this much endears God to an ingenuous heart, when he sees he has leave to drink not only at the stream, but at the fountain also; how that, as He is justified by the righteousness of Christ, so freely by grace, as the motive of this way of justification.

God is not moved by anything outside of Himself in our justification. As Moses said to the children of Israel, "The Lord set His love upon you because He loved you." And as our blessed Savior said to His Father, "I thank Thee, O Father, Lord of Heaven and Earth, because Thou hast hid these things from the wise and prudent, and hast revealed them unto babes; even so Father, for so it seemed good in Thy sight" (Matthew 11:25–26). Why does God justify a sinner by the righteousness of another (yet made ours)? Because it is His good pleasure so to do. For we were justified when ungodly (Romans 4:5), reconciled when we were sinners (Romans 5:10), loved when we were in our blood (Ezekiel 16:6), and Christ died for us when we were without strength (Romans 5:8).

Grace in the stream flows from grace in the fountain; our justification, adoption, calling, and glory all flow from the good will and pleasure of God. "Of His own good will hath He begotten us" (James 1:18). We are "predestinated according to the purpose of Him, who worketh all things after the counsel of His own will" (Ephesians 1:11). Paul says that our justification is reckoned of favor, and not of debt (Romans 4:4–5). He calls it a free gift: "The free gift is of many offenses unto justification." And also, "They which receive abundance of grace, and of the gift of righteousness" (Romans 5:17).

Yet for a right understanding of this point, we must know that this motive of our justification, the free grace of God, does not exclude the ransom of Christ, but takes it in. "Being justified freely by His grace, through the redemption that is in Christ Jesus" (Romans 3:24). And though it is never said that by our own obedience we are made righteous, yet it is said that by Christ's obedience we are: "By the obedience of one shall many be made righteous" (Romans 5:19).

There is a sweet accord between God's free grace and Christ's ransom in the justification of a sinner. The Socinians yield the one, free grace, but ungraciously exclude the other, Christ's ransom, they making Jesus Christ, in His life and death, only an exemplary good man and martyr, but not a propitiator or meritor for us. But if this is so, how much of the Scripture must we blot out? Nay, it subverts the whole fabric and design of God in man's recovery from his lost estate. As the apostle said in the case of the resurrection, we may say in this, "Then is our preaching in vain, and your faith in vain."

If any think that God's free grace is eclipsed by receiving a price for us in our justification, I answer, no, in no way; but rather the free grace of God more abundantly shines forth in Christ's ransom. As the apostle said, "Do we then make void the law through faith? God forbid, yea, we establish the law" (Romans 3:31). So we say, do we make void the free grace of God through Christ's ransom? No, but we rather establish it:

First, in His setting Christ apart for us as the Paschal Lamb, to be a sacrifice for our sins, to make Him capable of being the Lord our Righteousness, this was of God's free grace. Nothing more sets out God's love to us to be wonderful than our justification and salvation by Christ. "God so loved the world that He gave His only begotten Son" (John 3:16). Our ransom by Christ was of God's contriving: "A body hast Thou prepared Me" (Hebrews 10:5). So upon the matter, God satisfies God for the sinner, and in our justification pays Himself, as it were, with His own money.

Second, what Christ did for our justification comes to us through free grace; for how else would we have anything to do with it? There is the free grace of God in giving Jesus Christ to us as well as in giving Christ to die. The necessity of both is in us, but the motive of neither is. Our being in Christ is only of God's grace: "But of Him are ye in Christ Jesus" (1 Corinthians 1:30). And whatever Christ is to us, He is that of God, or through His grace: "Who of God is made unto us wisdom, and righteousness, and sanctification, and redemption." And, indeed, there is as much free grace discovered in our justification by Christ as if God had justified us without Him; yea, the discovery of free grace is greater the former way than the latter.

It is true, there is a paying of a price transacted between God and Christ, but betwixt God and us and Christ and us, all is free; it is a free gift. All that we do in our justification is to receive what He gives: "To as many as received Him, to them gave He power to be-

come the sons of God" (John 1:12). Our pardon is
bought by Christ, but comes freely to us.

There is a sweet consort between justice and free
grace in this way of a sinner's justification. The justice
of God is fully satisfied, and yet we are freely justified.
And that Christ shed blood for our pardon advances
free grace in that our pardon is sealed with such precious blood. Herein God commended His love to us, in
that "while we were yet sinners Christ died for us."
God's oath did not more confirm His promise to us
than the blood of Christ advanced His free grace in our
pardon. As this advances the grace of God, so it advances His justice, which had and must have satisfaction by such blood as Christ's. The active obedience of
Christ was not enough to expiate our sins without His
passive obedience also. His death as well as His life
must be offered for our price.

So when the whole sum is cast up, what does the
sinner contribute to his justification? Nothing but receiving it, which is called "faith" (and that is not his
own either, but a gift too). Our faith has nothing more
to do but to receive what is given. And our works, even
our best works, have nothing to do with it. "Who hath
saved us, and called us with a holy calling, not according to our works, but according to His own purpose
and grace which was given us in Christ Jesus" (2 Timothy 1:9). And Titus 3:5: "Not by works of righteousness
which we have done, but according to His mercy He
saved us."

Though Christ's works and God's free grace will
well consist together, yet our works and God's free
grace will not. "If it be of grace, then it is not of works,"
said Paul, "otherwise grace is no more grace" (Romans
11:6). They can no more mingle together than the iron
and clay in that great image spoken of in Daniel 2.

It is true, we must have works, holy works, and yet we must be justified without them. Romans 3:28: "We conclude therefore that a man is justified by faith, without the deeds of the law." Though justifying faith is not without works, yet it justifies without them. Works before faith cannot justify, for "without faith it is impossible to please God"; and works after faith do not justify, but proceed from a man already justified.

So that, turn every stone you can, you will find that the justification of a sinner is of free grace, and must be so, if we consider:

• That all other links of the golden chain in Romans 8:30 are acts of free grace—our predestination, our adoption, our calling, our glory—and why not then our justification? The apostle to the Ephesians says that election and adoption have their origin in "the good pleasure of His will." In sanctification God gives us both to will and to do, and that of His good pleasure— and why should not his own good pleasure have as much to do in our justifying righteousness? Certainly this is to the praise of the glory of His grace in Christ Jesus as well as the other.

• Upon what terms poor sinners are invited to Christ for righteousness and rest. This shows all freeness in God and in Christ in the case. We must come to Christ for righteousness and life, weary and oppressed with the sense of sin; and we must come poor and empty-handed, without money, and without price—and this shows that we have all of free grace.

• How God has purposely and carefully excluded all boasting on our part in our justification. He has left us no place for self-glorying: "Where is boasting then? It is excluded" (Romans 3:27). The reason why the Jew missed righteousness was because he went about to establish his own righteousness (Romans 10:3). God has so laid His plot and design in making sinners righteous that he who glories must glory in the Lord. All a man's own, even the best of all, must in this point be as zeroes. Though grace and holiness, holy duties and holy works, are of great price in the sight of God, in their due place, as Paul said of a meek and quiet spirit in Christian women, yet in the point of justification before God, they are but as zeroes. Here we must deny our best self as well as our worst.

5

Uses of the Doctrine

Now the uses of this particular, the great motive of a sinner being made righteous by the righteousness of Christ, that is, "the free grace of God," are these:

USE 1. This may persuade us to get a timely acquaintance with this righteousness of Christ made ours, in its fountain and great motive, the free gift of God. Let us remember that here is its origin. Christians are strange-spirited Christians till they are knowledgeable in this matter; therefore, acquaint yourselves well with free grace upon this account.

You will never sit fast, nor be in a settled state, until then. It is true, comfort and rejoicing comes in upon the view of your inherent grace and holy walking. "This is our rejoicing, the testimony of our conscience, that in simplicity and godly sincerity we have had our conversation in this world" (2 Corinthians 1:12). And you may not only refresh yourselves by your sincere and holy walking, but, to speak with reverence, you refresh God Himself. It is said by Moses, "God rested on the seventh day, and was refreshed" (Exodus 31:17); the phrase is fitted to our condition, as that in the next verse is, and many more of the like kind. Now as God is refreshed with His own holy day, so is He with the holy conversations of His own people. Their humble and sincere walking cheers both God and man, both Him and their own consciences; as the vine is said to do in that parabolic discourse in Judges 9. Enoch pleased

God in walking with Him, and knew he did so.

Aye, but though you may please God with this, yet you may not think to satisfy God with all this. He must have a bigger price for you than you yourselves can give. He could abate nothing of the life and death of Jesus Christ.

And then, further, there are such imperfections in your own grace and holiness that you know you lose the comfort of them many times by a temptation or two. Aye, but were you well acquainted with and versed in this righteousness of Christ reputed yours by favor and free grace, you would now feel yourselves upon a stone that lies fast, and upon a firmer rock than Mount Zion, which cannot be moved. Moved you may be, but not removed; your dependence is on an everlasting righteousness. While your eyes fix on yourselves and your own righteousness within doors, you will be as in a leaking vessel at sea, or as in those disciples' ship who cried, "Lord, save us, we perish." Christ must have the honor of justifying you as well as of saving them: and therefore you must count all you own but loss for him, as Paul did.

Oh, give me that to justify me before God that I can boast of, and with which I may outbrave death and hell, as blessed Paul did. Oh, spend your deep meditations on what is written in Isaiah 45:25: "In the Lord shall all the seed of Israel be justified and shall glory."

St. Paul dared not settle upon his own righteousness, even when at best: "I know nothing by myself, yet am I not hereby justified" (1 Corinthians 4:4). God can see that in you which you cannot see in yourselves. David owned this when he asked God to search him, and begged that God would cleanse him from secret sins.

What is the reason that many Christians are so un-fixed in their thoughts of themselves and their conditions, and are at such ebbs and flows in their opinion of their estates, but because their eye is more upon what is in them and what is done by them than what is in Christ and what He did for them; it is good to look at home, but not to rest here. Many men would partner with Christ's righteousness and God's free grace for their peace and comfort, but this is to have one foot on the firm ground and another in a boat, which is bad standing.

This spirit is too much like that mongrel righteousness of the Galatians, which they learned from false apostles. There is a natural tendency in us all to self-righteousness; but it is prejudicial to solid comfort. Christ's righteousness founded on free grace is the rock whereon we must build that peace which the rain and the winds cannot overturn. Free grace is the *primum mobile*, the primary vehicle that carries about all the degrees of our eternal salvation from first to last.

Some of the papists themselves will own this when they come to die. Witness Bellarmine's final statement: "It is the safest way to trust only to the merits of Christ for life and salvation." He said as much in a clause in his will. Cardinal Poole rigorously contended at the council of Trent (though in vain) for justification to be determined by faith alone. The theology in these mens' consciences was purer than that in their heads.

USE 2. Be well-versed in Christ's righteousness as founded in free grace, and it will be a good nurse to obedience and a godly life. The taste of free grace makes a man free to serve Christ and suffer for Him. If you would enlarge a straitened heart, get a taste of free grace. This brings all into tune in a Christian's spiritual motion. As Jonathan's tasting that honey (1 Samuel 14) quickened his sight, just so quickening will the taste of the free grace of God in Christ be to your minds in those duties that are incumbent on you.

USE 3. This gives great sinners an invitation to come to Christ for His righteousness. There is no price or money to be paid for it; it is of free grace; it's a free gift (Romans 5). And when such sinners have entertained it, the greater sinners they once were, the greater saints now they will be, as Paul was. And where sin has abounded, grace will much more abound. As it has abounded *to* them, so it will abound *in* them.

USE 4. This tells us what a generation of men they are who drink in this divinity the worst. They are those who are self-depending and self-ascribing; they are like him in Matthew 19:20: "All these have I kept from my youth," and whose question to Christ was, "What good thing shall I do that I may have eternal life?" They are like those self-boasting preachers in the Church of Corinth, as Luther usually calls them; and like him who thus answered Paul's question in 1 Corinthians 4:7 ("Who maketh thee to differ from another?"), "I myself make myself to differ."

This doctrine of Christ's righteousness laid on free grace is a doctrine that galls proud Christians and men of parts to the heart; such as trade for their own reputation with their parts and duties. To count all loss for Christ is as hard for them as it was to that rich man to lose all for Him.

But till a man can be content to be justified by a righteousness that is of free grace, he is not humbled enough in the sense of sin. To close this particular, remember, when you are to deal with God in the point of righteousness and justification, that you must leave all your own righteousness and duties, works and worth, at the foot of the mount, as Abraham did his servants when he went up to offer his son Isaac.

Thus we have seen the great moving cause in Christ's righteousness made ours, the free grace of God. And indeed we may say, Oh, what glorious grace is this! Were our justification put to sale upon our doing, then would we be in the tune of those desperate Jews, whose cry was, "There is no hope." Happy are we that free grace is the Alpha and Omega of all steps we take to eternal life. Election, redemption, justification, and all are pure donations.

6

God's Part in Making Christ's Righteousness Ours

How or in what manner does the righteousness of Christ becomes ours? It is another's righteousness; how then can another's be ours? This is the great case that remains to be discussed.

Now the truth of the matter is plain enough. "By the righteousness of one, the free gift came upon all to justification of life. By the obedience of one shall many be made righteous" (Romans 5:18–19). This righteousness in not a sinner's own; it is first the righteousness of another, and then made his, and must be so before it can justify him before God. The garments which made Jacob of so sweet a savor to his old father Isaac were not his own, they were his elder brother's; yet he had them on him. And this made his father say, "See, the smell of my son is as the smell of a field which the Lord hath blessed" (Genesis 27).

But how this comes about is the great inquiry. And here three things must be demonstrated:

1. The capacity of a sinner to have this righteousness of Christ made his.

2. What God does in making it ours.

3. What the sinner must do that this righteousness of Christ may be his.

1. A man's capacity for such propriety in Christ's righteousness is his union with Him. Christ's taking

44

our nature into union was His capacity to take our sins and condemnation on Himself; and His taking our persons into union is our capacity to have that interest in His righteousness so as to be made the righteousness of God in Him. The first union was for the second, and the second is for our capacity to receive the virtues and benefits of the first. Christ first espoused our natures, and then our persons; and hence comes in the wonderful sympathies that are between Christ and us: First, that He suffers with us (Acts 9:5; Matthew 25:45), and that He "cannot but be touched with the feeling of our infirmities" (Hebrews 4:15).

So we in this way suffer with Him, are justified in Him, are raised up together with Him, and are made to sit together in heavenly places in Him. Union is the ground of all the comfort and privilege we have by the Lord Jesus Christ. Our communion springs from our union with Him. Had we not been in the first Adam, we would not have sinned with him, nor derived sinfulness from him. The apostle speaks of this as an evident case. So if we are not in the second Adam, His righteousness and life cannot be communicated to us.

In a marriage union, the wife is honorable by her husband's honor; her debts become his and his estate and qualities hers. Thus it comes to pass by our union of espousals to Christ ("My Beloved is mine, and I am His.") that we have an interest and propriety in His merit and Spirit, in His righteousness and life. By the former espousals, that is, of our natures, He took our sins upon Him; by these espousals of our persons, we take His righteousness upon us. By marriage to Him, "All are yours, and you are Christ's" (1 Corinthians 3:22). So that Christ is to us not only a Head of eminence, as He is to the angels, but a Head of influence and communication, as the bridegroom is the bride. It is by this union of espousals that we are His love and

His undefiled. And here is the reason why the Father loves believers as He does Christ: "That the love wherewith thou hast loved me may be in them, and I in them" (John 17:26).

2. This righteousness of Christ is made ours, on God's part, by imputation. God counts it unto us for righteousness, and it is so, as the Scripture says, "Abraham believed God, and it was accounted to him for righteousness."

The Roman Catholics have made a great disturbance and insurrection against this blessed and sweet evangelical doctrine by violent and subtle reasonings for an infused and an inherent righteousness in us in the point of satisfaction. But it is a wonder that they should raise their dust in their own faces, and maintain argument where their own consciences oftentimes give them a rebuke, especially when they are upon the borders of the next world. I say they might be wondered at, were it not that they are blinded as well as the Jews in this case, and that the smoke from the bottomless pit disturbs their sight, and were it not that the judgment is upon them "because they received not the love of the truth that they might be saved. For this cause God shall send them strong delusions, that they should believe a lie" (2 Thessalonians 2:10). Yea, and it is no marvel that they so much contend for self-exalting divinity, whose head exalts himself above all that is called God.

But let us consider and weigh the case rationally, and then look how Christ was made sin for us in the same way are we made righteousness by Him. Now Christ was made sin for us by imputation, and not by inhesion of sin in Him. Christ had no sin in Him, nor did He sin; in these ways He knew no sin, as the apostle says to the Corinthians. But our sins were laid upon Him (Isaiah 53:6). Thus the righteousness of Christ that justifies us before God is not a righteousness of His in us, but a righteousness put upon us. "Thy beauty was perfect through My comeliness put upon thee, saith the Lord" (Ezekiel 16). And surely, as the one part of our justification, namely our discharge from condemnation, is done by God's not imputing sin to us (Psalm 32:2: "Blessed is the man to whom the Lord imputeth not sin"), not by having no sin in him, but by having no sin imputed to him, so the other part of justification, namely a man's being made righteous in the sight of God, is not by putting righteousness in him, but by imputing righteousness to him. Even as David described the blessedness of the man unto whom the Lord imputes righteousness without works.

The papists will not deny all imputed righteousness; but then they say that the righteousness which God imputes to us is inherent righteousness, grace within us. But how then does He justify the ungodly? How does He justify the sinner who has no grace? As I have before proved, justification finds men ungodly, though it does not leave them so. And, besides, herein they confound justification and sanctification, faith and works, the law and gospel, the first and second covenant. They are as bad, if not worse, than those Galatians whom the apostle charges for that very reason to have turned aside to "another gospel."

Doubtless, therefore, this doctrine that makes our justification before God to consist in inherent grace deserves to be exploded and blotted out forever from the church of God as one of those doctrines of men (Colossians 2:22), as that leaven and doctrine of the Pharisees our blessed Savior cautioned His disciples to beware of, and as the same with the doctrine of those perishing Jews who stumbled at that stumbling stone, namely, seeking after righteousness by something in themselves; which Paul called, "going about to establish their own righteousness."

And this leaven, or doctrine of the papists, deserves to be exploded by the church of God forever upon these, among many more, reasons:

• Because it derogates much from the glory of Christ; for it does not make His righteousness, but our own, the immediate reason of our justification. Christ, say the Romanists, merited that grace for us that is in us; and then this grace in us merits our justification, and for this God justifies us.

But is it not a wonder how that in us should merit of God which is imperfect and needs forgiveness? So our imperfections in grace need forgiveness as well as our sins. Why else has God ordained an office, a high priest, and such a one as Jesus Christ, to bear the iniquities of our holy things, as is evident in His type in this very case. Why now, if we have such grace and righteousness within us as may justify us and make us stand upon our own account in the pure sight of God, what need is there for this office of Christ? This generation of men pretend to give much to Christ, but they sift the matter and take infinitely more from Him. They take from Christ to give to grace in man.

We have owned, and still do, that inherent grace in the saints is a precious thing; one grain of it is worth a world, and is of great power and efficacy, as our Savior said of a grain of faith. But grace is set too high when we make it our righteousness. It is grace that is our righteousness before God, according to their doctrine, and not Christ. He loses this name, "The Lord Our Righteousness," if God justifies us for inherent grace: and so the order and platform of the whole gospel is spoiled and inverted. For as a natural man may be said to be *inversus decalogus,* the decalogue turned upside down, so this point of the papist's justification by inherent grace may as well be called *inversum evangelium,* the gospel turned upside down, or another gospel

(Galatians 1). For it is most certain that as we have imputed sin from the first Adam as well as inherent, and it was the imputed righteousness of the second Adam that brings us under justification of life, so to take away Christ's imputed righteousness is to take away much of His glory as Mediator.

• As it derogates much from the glory of Christ, so it takes much from the comfort of a Christian, who is often as much troubled and perplexed for the weakness of his grace as the strength of his sin, and so is fain to fly to Christ for sanctuary not only from his sins, but from the imperfection of his graces. So God's people did in the Old Testament, and so did they in the New: "Not having mine own righteousness, but that which is through the faith of Christ."

And truly, for all the dust the papists stir up in trying to make our justification to lie in inherent grace, as the matter of it, yet their consciences confute their doctrine when they come into trouble. Then you shall find purer divinity in men's consciences, when under the rebuke of God, than in their heads. When their champion Bellarmine came to the point of death, then in a few words he refuted and unsaid all that he had said and written in his life in this point of man's justification before God by his inherent grace. This you saw before. And show me the trembling conscience that ever fled to any other city of refuge than Christ's righteousness. It was Christ only who said, and could say, "Son, be of good cheer, thy sins are forgiven thee," and, "Woman, go in peace; thy faith, thy faith in Me, hath saved thee."

Such a man as Paul, for all his inherent grace, called himself a wretched man: and here was his last refuge: "I thank God through Jesus Christ our Lord," and, "There is therefore now no condemnation to them that are in Christ Jesus." You see that he gloried not in his own grace, but in Christ's.

OBJECTION. But did not Paul glory in his inherent grace, and the influence of it in his life, as the ground of rejoicing? "But our rejoicing is this, the testimony of our conscience, that in simplicity and godly sincerity we have had our conversation in the world" (2 Corinthians 1:12).

ANSWER. This passage of Paul's concerns his justification against the reproach of men, and not before God. False apostles and false brethren aspersed and disparaged him much, and charged him with things that he did not know. David's adversaries did just so by him in Psalm 35. Here Paul's good conscience he had lived in wiped off all this; their dirt would not stick on Paul; their foul breath slid off him, as a man's from the blade of a new knife or sword. "This is our rejoicing, the testimony of our conscience." This was his comfort, that though their mouths reproached him, yet his own heart did not.

But now, though the conscience of a godly man's sincerity will justify him to himself against the charge of men, yet he must have something else to satisfy his own conscience and to justify him before God. Observe therefore the reason of that famous challenge of Paul's: "Who shall lay any thing to the charge of God's elect? It is God that justifieth. Who is he that condemneth? It is Christ that died" (Romans 8:33). He does not say that they have inherent grace and gracious lives to answer for them, but that they have Christ who died, and Christ who rose again, and Christ who makes intercession for them to answer the charge. This is their bar against any charge to condemnation, and a screen between them and the wrath to come.

• The doctrine of the papists in this case deserves expunging because it makes such a confusion in the Scripture, and in the privileges of the saints. It confounds justification and sanctification, which the Scriptures make distant and different things and privileges. "Who of God is made unto us righteousness *and* sanctification" (1 Corinthians 1:30). And 1 Corinthians 6:11: "But ye are sanctified, but ye are justified." Sanctification is a thing that is inherent in us, but justification is a thing that is reckoned to us. "Abraham believed, and it was counted to him for righteousness" (Romans 4).

Moreover, they who are justified are equally so; it is not so with they who are sanctified. Adam's imputed sin was alike to all, and the guilt alike to all (Romans 5), but not so his derived and propagated sin; for this admits of more and less in men: some have more sin than others, as some have more grace than others. For sanctification is an inherent quality, and admits of degrees, as heat in water does; but justification is an act of relation, and does not admit of degrees. A child is no more a child at seven or seventeen years of age than he was the first day he was born. So when all these things are laid together, the opinion of the papists for justification by inherent grace must be rejected as spurious and foreign from Scripture: and justification by imputed righteousness is the truth to be received and adhered to.

QUESTION. But what is this imputing of righteousness to us?

ANSWER. As is God's not imputing sin to us, such is His imputing of righteousness. Now God's not imputing sin to us, which is spoken of by David and Paul (Psalm 32; 2 Corinthians 5:19; and Romans 4), is not because we have no sin, for that is not so, says 1 John, but because He charges us with none. Jeremiah 50:20: "The iniquities of Israel shall be sought for, and there shall be none," that is, none laid to their charge, "and the sins of Judah, and they shall not be found; for I will pardon them whom I reserve." And this may be the sense of those so greatly wrested words in Numbers 23:21: "He hath not beheld iniquity in Jacob, neither hath he seen perverseness in Israel," that is, He will impute none, but cover and pardon all, and so there is no hope that they should be cursed. The Lord blessed them in covering and not imputing their sins, and so Balaam could not curse them.

Thus God is said in Scripture to impute righteousness to them who believe, not because they have this righteousness in them, but because He reckons it as theirs, and reckons them righteous by it. "That we might be made the righteousness of God in Him." He became sin for us by imputation, not inhesion; we become righteousness through Him not by inhesion but by imputation.

Nor is this a fancy or fiction, but a real thing. For as our sins which deserved damnation were really laid on Christ by God, that is, in a law sense, as a debt is on a surety, though he had none of the money, so, in the same way, His righteousness is laid on us so as truly to be made ours. The Scripture says that God is "the Justifier of him that believeth in Jesus," and that "to him that worketh not, but believeth on Him that justifieth the ungodly, his faith is counted for righteousness."

So then, we see that it is not men's grace that He gives as the reason of their justification, but to a righteousness in Christ that is believed on. God covers your sins as he did David's in Psalm 32. With what does He do this? With your inherent grace? No, in no way; this is too narrow to do it. Your own righteousness will not cover your nakedness any better than Adam's leaves did his. Adam and Eve's nakedness was covered with a covering of God's providing (Genesis 3:21). The Lord said to His people, the Jews, "I spread My skirt over thee, and covered thy nakedness" (Ezekiel 16:8). As the law in the Ark was covered by the mercyseat, which was a figure of Christ, so our sins against the law are covered by Christ from the judging eye of God.

But here we are to consider by way of caution that though we are to distinguish between justification and sanctification, yet do we not, nor may we, separate or disjoin them. They go together in the same person as heat and light do in the sun. None are justified but they who are also sanctified. "But ye are sanctified, but ye are justified" (1 Corinthians 6:11), and "Whom He called, them He justified" (Romans 8:30). There is a conjunction of them, but no confusion.

Neither do we deny but that sanctification is called righteousness in Scripture. It is said of Zacharias and Elizabeth that they were both righteous before God (Luke 1:6). But how? With a righteousness of well-pleasing, such as Enoch's was (Hebrews 11:5), not with a meritorious righteousness which that must be which justifies a sinner; because none but such a righteousness can stop the mouth of the law and expiate the curse of it, which no righteousness can do but that righteousness of Christ which by imputation is made ours.

I shall add three confirmations that this righteousness of Christ is made ours by imputation:

From the figures and types that were of this thing in the ceremonial law. Consider how the sin of the offender in that law was transferred to the sacrifice or sin offering, and how the sins of all Israel were passed over to the goat. Were those legal offenses put into the goat? And were they inherent in him? It is an absurd thing to think so. But the offenses of the people were laid upon the sacrifice. "Aaron shall lay both his hands upon the head of the live goat, and confess over him all the iniquities of the children of Israel, and all their transgressions in all

their sins, putting them upon the head of the goat, and
so send him away into the wilderness" (Leviticus 16:21).
The same we find of the bullock in Leviticus 4:14–15.
Observe that the iniquities of the people were put upon
the sacrifice, not into it. This was, in a figure, this imputation, and so was an act of legal justice whereby the
offenders were discharged.

Now this is exactly answered in Christ. Our sins are
transferred to Him. How? Not *into* Him, but *upon* Him.
"The Lord hath laid *on* Him the iniquities of us all."
And so is His righteousness transferred to us. How? Not
by inhesion but by imputation; and so by a judicial act.
It is not put into us, but upon us. And surely it would
amount to blasphemy to say otherwise, that either our
sins for which He was condemned were in Him, or that
His righteousness for which we are justified is in us.
The Scripture speaks expressly upon both, as to the type
and antitype. The papists impute the supererrogating
works of a monk to another man, and yet will not allow
the imputation of Christ's to us!

From the parallel between the two Adams. The first Adam's
sin was ours. But how? Not inherently, but imputedly.
Now, as the first Adam's sin is ours, after the like manner is the second Adam's righteousness ours. Imputed
sin is taken away by imputed righteousness.

OBJECTION. But we have inherent sin both from
Adam and of our own also; and by what righteousness
are these done away?

ANSWER. By the same righteousness, for so the
apostle says plainly: "the free gift" of Romans 5:16, that
is, of righteousness, in verse 17 "is of many offenses
unto justification."

*From the consideration that no other grace is said in Scripture
to justify us but faith alone.* Not repentance, nor patience,
nor any other grace else, yet these are inherent graces
in us. But is not faith an inherent grace also? Yes, but

faith does not justify as it is a grace in us, but as it goes out of us and carries us out of ourselves, and as it lays hold on another righteousness than our own within us; namely Christ's obedience and blood in their merit. It is this way that faith justifies, which is not said of any other grace.

QUESTION. But if the blood and obedience of Christ justify, how does faith justify?

ANSWER. Faith is said to justify because of all graces it only is used in our justification. Faith applies that which justifies, which is the righteousness of Christ. The eye of an Israelite did not heal the place stung by serpents (Numbers 21) as it was one of the five senses, but as it looked up to the brazen serpent. So faith justifies a man not as it is one of the graces of the Spirit in him, but as it looks on Christ for justification, who is the antitype of that healing serpent. "As Moses lifted up the serpent in the wilderness, even so must the Son of man be lifted up" (John 3:14).

Thus we see that the righteousness which justifies us is not our own, and yet is made ours, not by inhesion in us, but by imputation to us. It is counted ours by our union with Christ; our marriage to Him gives us a title to His righteousness. And as Sarah called Abraham "Lord," so may we call Christ "The Lord Our Righteousness." God was not in our graces, but in Christ, reconciling us to Himself, not imputing our trespasses to us. Therefore holy Paul abased his own righteousness even as dung, as to any justifying power. And therefore the Scripture debased Abraham's work of grace in this point; though otherwise it makes them of high value. The Holy Ghost did thus by both those eminent saints to exclude boasting from both. And if from them, then from us much more

The papists object against this by saying that if I am righteous by the righteousness of Christ made mine, then I am as righteous as Christ Himself.

To this I answer that I and you are as righteous hereby as the righteousness of Christ needs to make us before God. The righteousness of Christ makes a believer as righteous as God would have him. And this may suffice, and be enough to him, without querying whether he is as righteous as Christ Himself.

Thus we have seen how Christ's righteousness becomes ours on God's part. It is by His imputing it to us that believe. It is by imputed righteousness that we are justified.

Now before I show what we must do that this righteousness may be ours, I shall make some application.

Here we are informed where our basis and foundation of comfort and glorying in God lies, even out of ourselves, and in what Christ is made unto us. When a poor soul is amazed by the charge of the law of God, and by the charge of his own conscience against him, and that not only for sin, but for weakness of grace and imperfections in his most gracious works, what is it that brings him out of this maze? What settles his disturbed concience and quiets his troubled spirit within him? Does his inherent grace? No, he complains of his graces as well as his sins; therefore this cannot do it. It must be something else that is better than his own grace and righteousness in him. And what can that be but the obedience and righteousness of Christ imputed to him? Paul had as little sin and as much grace as any man when in a state of grace; and yet he complained in both cases of the strength of sin and the weakness of grace. He bewailed it that he did the evil which he did not want to do, and that he did not the good he wanted to do. And notwithstanding all his grace, he cried out of himself, "O wretched man that I am, who shall deliver me?" My grace? No. "But I thank God through Jesus Christ our Lord." Here was his sanctuary and city of refuge; here his conscience had peace and rest.

Remember this, then, in your perplexities within, and when you cannot but esteem your own righteousness as filthy rags, that Christ has enough righteousness, and that He has it for you. As He said to His disciples, "Because I live, ye shall live also" (John 14:19), so, "because I have righteousness, ye shall have righteousness also" Isaiah 45:24: "Surely shall one say, 'In the Lord have I righteousness and strength.' " And it is such a righteousness as satisfies all the demands of God's justice and puts a sufficient bar between you and wrath and hell. "There is therefore now no condemnation to them that are in Christ Jesus." Jesus has delivered us "from the wrath to come."

Here is a righteousness too hard for your sins. "Where sin abounded, grace did much more abound. For if by the offense of one many be dead, much more by the grace of God, and the gift by grace, which is by one man Jesus Christ, hath abounded unto many" (Romans 5:20, 15). Oh, then, let the troubled conscience fly from the sins that pursue it to this securing righteousness. Yea, and if you are an experienced Christian, your experience tells you often that you are fain to fly from your grace because of its imperfection for sanctuary here. It is only this righteousness made yours that can scatter your fears and answer your objections. Here, your own experience tells you, is your safest and sweetest place of repose.

And, my brethren, take this advice: carry this cordial about in wearisome times, this name of Christ, "The Lord Our Righteousness." When the Lord would give Judah a sign of their rescue in their great straits, this was the sign: "Behold, a virgin shall conceive and bear a son, and shall call His name 'Emmanuel, God with us.' " (Isaiah 7:14). And this was to be a blessed sign to the same people in later troubles of their coming out, as in this text and context: "In His days Judah shall be saved, and Israel shall dwell safely. And [or "for"] this is His name whereby He shall be called: The Lord Our Righteousness. Therefore, behold the days to come, saith the Lord, that they shall no more say, 'The Lord liveth which brought up the children of Israel out of Egypt'; but, 'the Lord liveth which brought up the house of Israel out of the north country.' " The meaning is that the latter deliverance would be more signal and famous that the former.

So when we call the Lord Jesus *Jehovah Tsidkenu*, "The Lord Our Righteousness," we may also call him, *Jehovah Ropheka*, "The Lord That Healeth Thee," *Jehovah Shamma*, "The Lord Is There," *Jehovah Nisi*, "The Lord Is My Banner," and *Jehovah Jireh*, "The Lord Will Provide," or, "In the mount of the Lord it shall be seen." The mountain of slaughter shall turn the mountain of deliverance; where Isaac should have been sacrificed, there Isaac was miraculously saved.

You must know that the righteousness that Christ is to us was from the merit and value of His blood. By this He overcame our sins, and the death and wrath that were due to them. And it is by this blood that the saints shall overcome the wrath of the devil. By this blood the church shall be secured from all her flesh and blood enemies. That which has borne the wrath of God, and overcome the wrath of the devil, will overcome with ease the wrath of man.

That righteousness that Christ is to us is a breastplate indeed; the words are quoted from Isaiah 59:16–17: "And he saw that there was no man, and wondered that there was no intercessor, therefore his arm brought salvation unto him, and his righteousness it sustained him, for he put on righteousness as a breastplate." You know the heart is in the breast; therefore this breastplate can secure the heart from trouble. "Let not your heart be troubled, ye believe in God, believe also in Me" (John 14:1). This was spoken to them when they were upon the confines of suffering for Christ.

And doubtless faith in Christ as "The Lord Our Righteousness" is a refuge and place of retreat from any storms. And observe that faith in Christ then, when He was at lowest and ready to be cut off, and descending into hell, was able to do this; how much more may faith in Christ do it now when He is in heaven, and when all power in heaven and earth is in His hands. Well may we receive this charge now, "Let not your heart be troubled, believe in Me."

Lastly, here is a place for glorying when we come to die. There are two special seasons wherein this name of Christ, "The Lord Our Righteousness," will be of great value to us: in trouble of conscience and at our death. In trouble of conscience this, if applied, will bid us be of good cheer, for our sins are forgiven us. Upon a death bed this righteousness will make a believer able to make two brave challenges. The first is found in Romans 8:33–34: "Who shall lay anything to the charge of God's elect? It is God that justifieth. Who is he that condemneth? It is Christ that died, yea, rather, that is risen again, who is even at the right hand of God, who also maketh intercession for us." The second is found in 1 Corinthians 15:55–57: "O death, where is thy sting? O grave, where is thy victory? The sting of death is sin; and the strength of sin is the law. But thanks be to God which giveth us the victory through our Lord Jesus Christ."

7

The Sinner's Part in Making Christ's Righteousness His Own

I now intend to show what the poor sinner must do so that this righteousness of Christ's may be made his, that he may call it his own, and use it as a bar against wrath and condemnation for sin, and as his title to life and glory.

We find that when sinners have been smitten in conscience and had wounds or pricks there, they have asked the question, and this has been their great query: "Men and brethren, what shall we do? Sirs, what must I do to be saved?" And the answer has always been this: "Believe in the Lord Jesus Christ." So that it is believing in Christ that makes a sinner righteous. "To him that believeth, his faith is counted for righteousness." Faith is the great and only instrument in man that God is pleased to use in transplanting Christ's righteousness to him. In Romans 4:11, it is called "the righteousness of faith." And Philippians 3:9 speaks of the "righteousness which is through the faith of Christ" and "the righteousness which is of God by faith."

Observe, it is called the faith of Christ and the faith of God: the faith of Christ because Christ and His righteousness is the object of it; the faith of God because He and His power only is the Author of it. No power but that of God, yea, that exceeding great and mighty power of God which raised Christ from the dead, can work faith in us (Ephesians 1:19–20).

QUESTION. But we find different answers given in Scripture to the question, "What shall I do to be saved?" For when that rich man asked Jesus the question, He sent him to the law: "If thou wilt enter into life, keep the commandments." And when the Jews who were pricked in their hearts put this question to the Apostle Peter, he answered "Repent." Paul bid the Philippian jailer who asked the same question, "Believe in the Lord Jesus."

ANSWER. These different answers to this self-same question were suited to the different tempers of the questioners. Jesus sent the rich man to the law because his heart was high and proud; he was an unhumbled man, and so fit to be sent to the law, there to be schooled first. The law is a schoolmaster to lead men to Christ. The moral law as well as the ceremonial points men to Christ, as the shadow to the substance: and that drives men to Christ by the perfect obedience it requires, and the great curse it denounces upon default. A man must come out of himself before he can come to Christ, and the law has a hand in this.

St. Peter bade the Jews, upon the question to repent because they had had their hands so lately in Christ's blood, and so their sin needed very deep humiliation before they could believe in Christ for pardon; and he does not bid them rest in repentance, but then sends them to faith in Christ.

Paul and Silas sent the poor, trembling jailer immediately to Christ. "Believe on the Lord Jesus Christ, and thou shalt be saved" (Acts 16:30–31). They did this because they saw that he was indeed a melted and a kindly humbled sinner. The two former are sent to Christ mediately, but this man was sent immediately.

The question being answered, I now proceed to the point under consideration, that it is faith on the sinner's part which brings Christ's righteousness home to him as his own. Christ Himself taught this point implicitly in His constant calling for faith from them whom He healed of bodily distempers.

For if faith in Christ is necessary to heal the body, much more is it necessary in the cure of the soul. It's useful to note how all those various phrases in Scripture, of men's looking upon Christ, receiving Christ, coming to Christ, eating and drinking Christ, all mean and intend their believing in Him.

And it is further to be noted that the gospel command is to believe in Christ: "And this is His commandment, that we should believe on the name of His Son Jesus Christ" (1 John 3:23). Also, the promises of the gospel are to believing persons: "Therefore it is of faith that the promise might be sure to all the seed, even that that is of the faith of Abraham" (Romans 4:16). Your comforts of the gospel come into the soul by believing: "In whom, though you see Him not, yet believing, ye rejoice with joy unspeakable and full of glory" (1 Peter 1:8).

Yet further, in our justification, the Scripture cries down works and exalts believing: "To him that worketh not, but believeth, is righteousness counted" (Romans 4:5). Yea, this believing in Christ silences all other graces in this point of justifying righteousness. It is not repentance, patience, love, prayer, or obedience that justifies us, but faith in Christ.

The ordinances of the ceremonial law, when compared with their gospel substances, are called weak and beggarly elements and carnal ordinances (Galatians 4:9; Hebrews 9:10) by the apostle; and this though they were the holy ordinances of God in their time. So are the best works and highest actings of grace when compared with the righteousness of Christ. That is why, comparatively, Paul counted the best of his own righteousness but dross.

It is for certain that in sanctification, though not justification, the saint's other graces and good works bear their part, keep their place, and are of great price in the sight of God, as Peter said of a meek and quiet spirit. Indeed, the lowest gracious action is of greater value than the most specious works of all ungracious men in the world. Even a cup of cold water given to a disciple in the name of Christ is more than a man's giving all his goods to feed the poor if he does not have charity. We know that Jesus Christ set a higher rate on the widow's two mites than on all the other treasure which was cast in (Mark 12:42).

And yet, though our graces and gracious works are of so great a price in the sight of God in their station and sphere, as we are sanctified persons, set apart for God Himself to be a kind of first-fruits of His creatures, to be holiness to the Lord and the first-fruits of His increase, yet, in the matter of our justification, they are all zeroes. Faith is the only thing in us and of ours that justifies—not that faith is a better grace than other graces, but because it has a better office. A constable in a town, or a justice of the peace in a country, may do that which another man, though as good as himself except for his office, cannot do; it is the office that makes the difference in this particular case.

So it is with faith and other graces. Looking on faith only as a grace, other graces equalize it; yea, the grace of love exceeds it in breadth and in length. Love exceeds faith in breadth, for faith is a personal grace; it is for a man's own use. A man cannot believe to life for another. But love is a public and communcative grace. The love of one Christian may extend to a thousand more, and for this reason it has the pre-eminence given it over faith.

Love exceeds faith in length. Love abides forever; it is the grace of the saints in heaven. "Now abideth faith, hope, and charity, these three, but the greatest of these is charity" (1 Corinthians 13:13). Faith and hope end with this life, as to their employment; but love is the working grace in the life to come. Faith and hope will be swallowed up, whereas love, which shone but as a star here, will be as a sun in heaven.

But consider faith in its office between Christ and a poor sinner in his reconciliation to God and his justification before Him. Faith has the pre-eminence of all other graces, and none have an office here but faith.

Now, to show the office and worth of faith in bringing home the righteousness of Christ to us for our righteousness before God, these two things must be opened: First, what object it is that faith acts on in our justification; and, second, what act of faith it is that justifies us.

First, the object of faith in general is the whole Scripture, or revealed written will of God. The authority of God is the reason for our believing. Our faith is not nor can be as large as God's mouth. "Whatever He bids you do, do it," said our Savior's mother to the waiters at the feast (John 2). So whatever God speaks, we must believe. It is impossible that God should lie (Hebrews 6:18).

But though this is the object of faith, yet it is not the object of faith that justifies; that is a particular and peculiar object. A man has sense and motion as well as reason, yet it's reason alone that makes him a man. Thus justifying faith believes all truths in Scripture, yet that does not justify unless it believes some particular truth or promise, the promise of Christ. What was the object of Abraham's faith that justified him? Why, it was the promise. What promise? The promise of a seed. And what seed? Christ. Galatians 3:16: "And to thy seed, which is Christ."

Abraham was not justified by his faith, as he believed the temporal seed promised to him, but the spiritual seed, Christ, who was the son of David, the son of Abraham (Matthew 1:1). Therefore it is observable that the apostle distinguishes subtly and punctually in this point upon one letter, the letter "s": "Now to Abraham and his seed were the promises made; he saith not to seeds, as to many, but as of one, and to thy seed, which is Christ." So there is a single, proper, and peculiar object of faith that justifies a sinner and makes him righteous, and that is Christ held forth by God in His active and passive obedience, in His life and death, to be the justification of a sinner. Christ held forth to us in the promise, made sin for us and righteousness to us, the diamond of the ring and the center of all parts of Scripture. To this the ceremonial and moral law pointed; to this the prophets and apostles refer a sinner as his sanctuary and city of refuge.

Though an Israelite who was bitten by the serpent had looked on the tabernacle and the holy things of God there, those would not have cured him; only his looking up to the brazen serpent could do it because only that was assigned by God as a remedy. So, though a sinner believes all other passages and points in the Scriptures, yet it is not this faith that will justify him, but his looking on Christ and believing on Him, as He was lifted up on the cross, there bearing our sins and transmitting the merit of His death to us—this is the faith that justifies.

Suppose a man of a troubled spirit and an afflicted conscience should believe all the commandments, and believe them to be holy, just, and good, as the apostle says in Romans 7. Surely this would not settle his disturbed conscience and give him peace. A poor soul's peace with God is through our Lord Jesus Christ, and faith in Him. This, therefore, may end all controversies as to what object of faith it is that justifies a sinner: it is only faith in Christ for righteousness that does it.

Second, what act of faith is it that justifies? It must be faith acted upon its proper and designed object for this end; for faith, being an instrument, must be used as an instrument or else it is not useful to its end. A knife, ax, or plaster are all useless unless they are actuated.

A Jew might have a working eye, and yet not be cured of his wound from the fiery serpent unless he looked up with his eye to the brazen serpent. That woman in Matthew 9 who was diseased with an issue of blood was not healed till she touched Christ's garments. So faith must act if it is to do a man good. Faith justifies a sinner by its acts, not its habit. It's not the habit, but the act of faith that justifies.

QUESTION. But are we not justified in God's decree before we believe?

ANSWER. We were elected to be justified, yes, but to be justified by faith, and not before. We were redeemed before we believed. Our faith gives nothing to the value of Christ's ransom with God; but it's faith that makes this ransom of Christ's to be mine.

God's acts of grace to sinners must be looked on in their order. It is said of the resurrection that "all shall be made alive in Christ, but every man in his own order: first Christ, then they that are Christ's" (1 Corinthians 15:23). So it is in this case: first we are to look upon Christ's paying our ransom and God's acceptance of it, and this is done before faith. Then we are to look upon God's imputing this ransom to us, and this He does not do till we believe. So if we consider justification in its contract between God and Christ, this is done before faith; for faith itself is in the ransom and purchase. But if we consider God's actual justifying of us, this is not done before faith. "Being justified by faith, we have peace with God," says Romans 5. We must be in Christ, and Christ in us, by faith before we are discharged of the sentence of condemnation.

Though Christ took our infirmities and bore our sicknesses, yet He cured none without faith. In the centurion's servant's sickness, "As thou hast believed, so be it done unto thee" (Matthew 8:13). So when the man brought his son to Christ to be cured, Christ pressed upon faith: "If thou canst believe" (Mark 9:23). So Christ bore our sins, yet we must believe in Him before our sins are pardoned. In Luke 7:48–50, "Thy sins are forgiven thee" and "thy faith hath saved thee" are joined together.

So though redemption was before faith, yet justification, which is God's imputing or applying this redemption to us, is not till faith. As the apostle said in Galatians 3:23: "Before faith came, we were kept under the law, being shut up unto the faith which should afterwards be revealed."

Nor does this make faith to be a meritorious condition in our justification; for God covenanted with Christ to give us that faith whereby we are justified. But faith is only an instrument which God is pleased to use in applying the plaster to the sore.

But the faith that thus justifies is not a bare assent to the promise of Christ; it's more than that. It is an act of the will and affections as well as of the understanding, an act of the heart as well as the head. "With the heart man believeth unto righteousness" (Romans 10:10). So that act of faith which justifies is an embracing act of faith. "To as many as received Him, to them gave He power to become the sons of God, even to as many as believed on His name" (John 1:12).

It is not the justifying act of faith to be assured that our sins are pardoned and that we shall be saved. This is the comforting act of faith, but not the justifying act. It is not the reflex act, but the direct act of faith that jus-

tifies us. The reflex act, which is assurance of our justification, is the effect of the other. A man may be justified by believing, though he does not have the sense of
his justification.

And so that act of faith in Paul where he declared
that Christ loved him and gave Himself for him
(Galatians 2:20) was a reflex act of faith, an effect and
fruit of that act of faith whereby he was justified. But
those acts of faith whereby he declared, "We have believed in Jesus Christ that we might be justified by the
faith of Jesus" (Galatians 2:16), and "Believe on the
Lord Jesus Christ and thou shalt be saved" (Acts 16:31),
were acts of faith. But what acts? Acts of adherence to
Christ for justification, and not acts of evidence that he
was already justified.

Neither does faith justify even as it acts and works by
love. Justifying faith does act by love, but it does not justify because it acts thus, nor as it acts and works in obedience. Faith does act thus, and therefore it is called
"the obedience of faith" in Romans 16:26. It was by faith
that Enoch walked with God (Genesis 5:24). It was by
faith that Abraham obeyed the commandment of God
in going out of his own country (Hebrews 11:8), not
knowing where he went; and it was by faith that he
offered up Isaac when he was commanded to do so by
God (v. 17). But these were not justifying acts of faith.
These are indeed the natural and necessary effects of
justifying faith. "Faith, if it have not works, is dead"
(James 2:17). And "I will show you my faith by my works"
(v. 18); but these acts of faith do not justify us.

The act of justifying faith, or the act of faith that justifies, is an act of relying and reliance on Christ as he
was made sin for us, and as He is made righteousness to
us, and thus offered by the Scripture to our faith. That
phrase of Scripture in 1 Peter 2:6 clears this: "Behold, I
lay in Zion a chief cornerstone, elect and precious, and

he that believeth on Him shall not be confounded."
What, believe on a stone? The meaning is that he who
rests upon this stone with all his weight, who lays his
whole stress of salvation here.

And this indeed is the justifying act of faith, when
the wounded sinner and perplexed conscience sees
Christ offered to him in the promise of God's free
grace to be this only and whole redemption and righteousness, and lays hold of Him thus offered, clasps
and embraces Christ thus offered, as the woman in
Matthew 28 did His feet. This, and this only, is the act
of faith that justifies. And here the weary soul rests itself
and experiences the truth of that Scripture, those words
of Christ, "Come unto Me, all ye that labor and are
heavy laden, and I will give you rest" (Matthew 11:28).
This is the horn of the altar. A poor humbled sinner, in
the sense of his own lost condition, flies to and holds
by, and says, as Joab did, "If I die, I'll die here" (1 Kings
2:30).

Yet you must note that this act of faith which lies in
a relying and resting on Christ alone for righteousness
is, in the New Testament, set out by the phrase
"believing into Christ," which we translate "believing
in Christ." For it signifies such an act or work of faith
and affiance in Christ whereby the soul is engrafted in
Him and united to Him, so that by this union it has
communion in this righteousness. And thus we see
that the gospel has brought the justifying act of faith
into a little room within this compass.

A convinced and humbled sinner's recumbing and
relying on the Lord Jesus Christ as offered in the
promise of free grace for his righteousness is the
ground of comfort, and of a believer's boasting over all
charges when he thus believes. He may now say with
the apostle, "Who shall lay anything to my charge? It is
God who justifies. Who shall condemn me? It is Christ

who died again, and He was raised again for my justification!"

In this believing we set our seal that God is true; and God will, in due time, if He has not done so already, set His seal to work assurance in you, to second your reliance. "But if you believe not, thus you make God a liar" (1 John 5:10).

Though you assent to the truth of the promises of Christ, yet if you draw back your affiance and relying, as if the promises were not to you, you give God the lie. Oh, then, in the sense of your own nakedness, come out of yourselves and cast yourselves on Christ for righteousness—and this is the faith that saves you.

How many men deceive themselves in this saving act of faith! If they know the promise of Christ as our righteousness and assent to it, they think that is enough. But, alas, it is not; for there must be a stripping of a man's self naked of his own righteousness and a resting on this righteousness of Christ's alone. David stripped himself of his armor, and so went out against Goliath in the name of the Lord. Adam was naked and saw it before God made the promise of Christ.

QUESTION. But is a man justified by this act of faith only? The papists ask us where this word "only" is in Scripture, and tell us that it is adding to Scripture.

ANSWER. It is in the sense of Scripture, though not in the letter of Scripture. This was a rule of the ancients, that the sense, and not the letter, is Scripture. Our blessed Savior did not add to the Scripture "Thou shalt fear the Lord thy God, and shalt serve Him" (Deuteronomy 6:13) when he said, "It is written, Thou shalt worship the Lord thy God, and Him only shalt thou serve" (Matthew 4:10). For though "only" is not in the letter of the text He quoted, yet it is in the sense; therefore Christ used it. Nor did the devil tax Him for

adding to the Scripture herein because it was the meaning of the text. We shall therefore open these two
things here: First, the true meaning of this, when we
say "this act of faith, this act of relying and reliance
alone justifies. Then, second, we will see to the ground
and reason of it, why this act of faith is counted by God
to a man for righteousness.

1. When we say that faith alone justifies, we mean
that all, even the best of all, in a man, or that which is
done by a man, is hereby excluded from his justification; yea, every act of faith, besides this one of relying
on Christ for righteousness, is excluded.

So this word "only" or "alone" excludes all inherent
grace, though in the highest measure, and all actual
holiness in a man's life or duties which have the greatest spirituality in them, even every fruit of the spirit but
this one of faith, and every act of faith besides this one
of reliance, are excluded from his justification before
God. This act of faith allows for nothing but the righteousness of Christ, and God's imputing it to a man.

It's true, there are other acts of a justifying faith besides that one which justifies. There is an act of faith
that purifies the heart, an act of faith that works by love,
and an act of faith that resists temptation (Acts 15:9;
Galatians 5:6; 1 John 5:4). "Moses, by faith, refused to be
called the son of Pharaoh's daughter, choosing rather
to suffer affliction with the people of God than to enjoy
the pleasures of sin for a season" (Hebrews 11:24–25).
And of other believers it is said (v. 35) that "by faith they
accepted not deliverance when tortured," that is, upon
unbecoming terms. These acts of faith are not excluded
from the justified believer, but from the act of faith in
justification they are.

When we say that faith alone justifies, we do not intend that faith has no other act or operation but to justify, but rather that nothing has the office to justify a

sinner but faith, and this act of faith, or reliance on the righteousness of Christ.

The eye of an Israelite could and did do other things besides look up to the brazen serpent; yet the eye did not heal by anything else it did but this. So faith, saving faith, has other business and work than this of looking to Christ for righteousness, but it makes a man righteous in no other way but this.

Therefore, we say that there are other graces coexistent with faith in the justified person. A solitary faith is not a saving and justifying faith. "Faith, if it hath not works, is dead, being alone" (James 2:17). Faith that is alone does not save, though faith alone saves. The act of seeing is by the eye only, without the ear or other senses; the eye alone sees. The ear does not see, nor taste, nor smell, nor feel; yet the eye could not see if you were to take away the other senses from the body.

So it is faith alone that justifies without other graces or good works; yet faith without them, or separated from them, cannot justify because, indeed, it cannot be without them in the person or subject where it is. So faith is without other graces in its office, but not in its existence. You may as soon part light and heat in the sun as sanctification from justification in a believer; for faith is not only a fruit of the Spirit, with other graces, but also the seed and nursery of other graces because faith in Christ is the root-grace. It was by faith that Enoch walked with God and that Paul did so dearly love Jesus Christ; it was by faith that the saints in both testaments prayed so much. "We believe, therefore do we speak" (2 Corinthians 4:13).

It would be a strange soul that should give a faculty of seeing and no other faculty or sense. And just as strange a state of grace would that be that should give an act of saving and justifying faith, and give no other graces besides.

What we say of other graces, we also say of gracious works: these cannot be severed from a justified person or from a justifying faith, though they have no office in his justification; for these justify faith as faith justifies the person.

And this is the exposition of James 2:21–22: "Was not Abraham our Father justified by works when he had offered Isaac? Seest thou how faith wrought with his works, and by works was faith made perfect." And the Scripture was fulfilled which said, "Abraham believed, and it was counted unto him for righteousness" (Genesis 15:6). And James 2:24: "Ye see, then, how that a man is justified by works, and not by faith only."

But how is that? And how do Paul and James agree, or even James with himself? The sense is that a man is not justified by a faith that is without works. "Abraham believed, and it was counted to him for righteousness," but then Abraham's believing was a working believing; it make him go out of his own country he knew not where upon God's call, and to offer up his son Isaac at God's command. This latter work of his is what James speaks of; and you must understand that this excellent work of Abraham's was more than thirty years after his justification. This appears by Scripture chronology, for in Genesis 15:6 we read that his believing was counted to him for righteousness, and his offering of Isaac in Genesis 22 was 30 to 40 years or more after that, says Bishop [James] Ussher.

So this must be the Apostle James' meaning when he says that Abraham was justified by works; this and no other can be the meaning without allowing for contradictions and strange inconsistencies: Abraham's faith was not without works, but was justified by his works to be a true faith, a living faith, and a saving faith. Abraham's person was justified by faith, and his faith was justified by works, specifically by offering up Isaac at God's command, which is what James speaks of.

So much for the expressions that "faith alone" justifies us, or makes Christ's righteousness ours.

But now we must be cautioned not to make or imagine the act of believing to be the matter of our righteousness, as some have held. For this is to make our faith our Christ, and to thrust out His righteousness from being the reason and matter of our justification. Faith is the only instrument of our righteousness, and this is honor enough. To make it more would be to make the virtue that healed the woman in Matthew 9 to come out of the hand that touched Christ's garments, and not out of Christ who was touched. It would be to make the healing virtue to be in the eye of an Israelite, and not in the brazen serpent that the eye beheld. These men would make us eat our money and not to buy bread to eat with it. They make faith our righteousness, which is but instrumental to make Christ the Lord our righteousness. And this is sufficient honor to faith; it needs claim no more, nor do we give it any more.

2. The ground or reason why faith alone justifies a sinner:

• The reason why God has dignified faith with this high office, and the reason why faith alone justifies, is to exclude boasting. Romans 3:27: "Where is boasting then? It is excluded. By what law? Of works? Nay, but by the law of faith." The Scripture is clear that we are justified by faith and not by works. "Not by works of the law," said the apostle. "Not by my own righteousness, but that of Christ made mine by faith" (see Philippians 3:7–9).

Again, nothing is said in Scripture to be imputed for righteousness but faith. "Abraham believed, and it was counted unto him for righteousness" (Genesis 15 and James 2:23). It was not Abraham's going out of his own country, nor Abraham's offering his son, but Abraham's faith that was imputed to him for righteousness. "To declare His righteousness, and that He is just and the Justifier of him that believeth in Jesus" (Romans 3:26).

Faith and unbelief are the two casting points of every man's present and final state. John 3:18: "He that believeth on Him is not condemned, but he that believeth not is condemned already, because he hath not believed in the name of the only begotten Son of God." So (v. 36), "he that believeth on the Son hath everlasting life; and he that believeth not the Son shall not see life." Faith is the only grace that actually saves, and unbelief is the only sin that actually damns.

• Another reason why faith alone justifies is because there is a suitableness in this grace of faith to God's plot and design in His way of justifying man. God, having made a different covenant with His people from that of works, the covenant of grace, it is convenient that whatever is required of us in this covenant be consistent with a covenant of free grace. Now faith is a grace of convenience because it takes all of free grace that God gives in order to obtain salvation.

God's free grace and our faith sweetly agree: "By grace are ye saved through faith." Free grace and our works do not accord: "Therefore it is of faith that it might be of grace; and if of grace, then it is no more of works, otherwise grace is no more grace" (Romans 4:16, 11:6). And, as I said before, it is of grace because God is resolved to exclude boasting from man, which could not be but by taking faith and excluding works in justification.

God found the disposition of man to incline to self-will and self-righteousness in his breach of the first covenant; and this is in man's nature still: "They, going about to establish their own righteousness, have not submitted to the righteousness of God" (Romans 10:3).

Therefore, God has made another kind of covenant with us, a covenant of free grace; and we must have what we have of free grace, and that it may be by grace it must be by faith. Faith and works are always set at variance by Paul in our justification before God. Faith is the sympathizing grace in us with the free grace of God. It is of faith that it may be of grace. Any way of boasting is cut off from man, and he who glories must glory in the Lord (1 Corinthians 1:31).

• God's intention of honoring the Lord Jesus Christ and making him a glorious Adam, wonderfully excelling the first one, is another reason why the justification of a sinner is only by faith in Christ. If we consider the scope of much of Romans 5:15–21 and of some parts of 1 Corinthians 15:45, we find a design of God to highly exalt the second Adam above the first.

Now faith is the grace that honors Christ most. It fetches all from Christ and gives all the blessedness of a restored sinner to Christ. It's faith that makes Christ so precious: "To you that believe, He is precious" (1 Peter 2:7). Faith makes the worst of Christ to be better and more eligible than the best of this world. It was by faith that Moses esteemed the reproaches of Christ greater riches than the treasure of Egypt. And because faith so honors Christ, therefore it is exalted above other graces to this high office, which no other grace has in the justification and righteousness of a sinner. It's faith that puts Christ's worth and merit into the balance against all your sins and wretchedness, against the curse of the law, and against (and to swallow up) hell and death into victory.

Faith makes a man to cast away not only his sins, but his own righteousness too, to exalt the righteousness of Christ. It makes a man's best duties, best works, and highest measures of inherent grace to be, in comparison to Christ's obedience and righteousness, but as stars to the sun, which disappear when the sun rises.

• The Lord has thus honored faith and set it in so high an office for His people's sake, that they may be at a certainty for their spiritual and eternal condition, and not in a tottering state, as they were in the first Adam.

All that God has for us regarding our eternal happiness He has put into Christ: "It pleased the Father that in Him should all fullness dwell" (Colossians 1:19). And it is from His fullness that we receive all grace; and what we have from the fullness of Christ, we fetch by faith, as the woman fetched virtue to heal her sore distemper. All this is that we may have certainty. Therefore it is of faith "to the end that the promise might be sure" (Romans 4:16). Faith leans upon Christ as its special object, and Christ is a sure foundation. "All the promises of God in Him are 'yea' and in Him 'Amen.' " There they have both their existence and performance (2 Corinthians 1:20).

If life and heaven hung upon such hinges as our own graces, works, and righteousness, we would be in a tottering case. We are so uncertain in these as to their actings, and withal so imperfect. But in Christ's obedience and righteousness there is the greatest assurance that can be. We may rest and repose here safely. He is a sure foundation where the conscience of a sinner can rest quietly, and nowhere else.

8

The Application

You have seen it proved and cleared that the Lord Jesus Christ is a sinner's righteousness in the sight of God, that God imputes this righteousness to a sinner to make it his, and that faith alone has the office to fetch it home and apply it. We now move to the application.

USE OF LAMENTATION. If these things are as you have seen, then, to use the Prophet Ezekiel's words, this is a lamentation, and shall be for a lamentation, that so much of the world is so ignorant of and are enemies to this foundational truth.

First, as to the Gentiles, they knew nothing of this righteousness until they were taught it by the grace of God in their calling. And not only the common people, but their *Sophoi*, their learned and wise men, their seers, such as Cato, Cicero, Ovid, Virgil, Livie, Suetonius, and more, men of high parts, who all lived about Christ's time, either a little before or a little after, all these were strangers, yea, enemies to this righteousness. Christ crucified was foolishness to them. It was a jeering speech of Cato's: "It is foolishness to look for any salvation after death." The wisest of the Gentiles no more understood the mystery of this righteousness which makes a sinner righteous before God, or any other of the mysteries of Christ, than the magi of Egypt did Pharaoh's dreams or the wisemen of Chaldea understood Nebuchadnezzar's or Belshazzar's handwriting. This masterpiece of wisdom in God was but foolishness to them.

Second, as for the Jews, Paul says that they were ignorant of this righteousness: "For they, being ignorant of God's righteousness, and going about to establish their own righteousness, have not submitted themselves to the righteousness of God" (Romans 10:3). Yea, this righteousness was a stumblingblock to them, an occasion of their fall and casting off, that is, through their ignorance of it and their malice against it; they stumbled at this stumbling stone (Romans 9:31–33).

And this was the plague-sore not only of the common people among the Jews, but of their rabbis, their scribes and teachers. They were ignorant, and willingly ignorant, of this way to life: "Have any of the rulers or of the Pharisees believed on Him?" (John 7:48).

Third, as for Christians, multitudes of them are ignorant of and bitter enemies to this righteousness. The generality of the Roman church have drunk this poison, and not a few of their champions are behind the scribes and Pharisees in contending for righteousness by the works of the law. They are rich enough to buy pardon of sins, and heaven too. What did Vega say but that he would have heaven for his money? And, indeed, all men by nature have this popery in their belly. And there are two reasons why men naturally and generally miss this way to life, this way to the city of refuge set up for lost sinners by the gospel:

1. The mysterious nature of this righteousness, as it is the matter and reason of a sinner's justification before God. It is a revelation: "The righteousness of God is revealed from faith to faith" (Romans 1:17). It is not a thing in the view of natural reason. The world must be convinced of it by the Spirit. It is a new way (Hebrews 10:20), an uncouth, untrodden, and unbeaten way to the light of nature; nay, there was no such thing known of in the state of innocence. Those philosophers, the Epicureans and Stoics who encountered Paul in Acts 17

called it "new doctrine." It is news indeed; so is the
whole gospel, for that is the sense of *evangelioi,* bringing
good news. Man being made righteous by the righteousness of another is a new way, and unknown to the
generality of the world, as America was to other parts
till of late.

That a righteous person should be made sin for us,
as Christ was, and that we should be made "the righteousness of God in Him," is a great mystery. And in
preaching this point to men, we may say, as the apostle
said about the resurrection, "Behold, I show you a mystery" (1 Corinthians 15:51). This is one of the deep
things of God, which no man knows but the Spirit of
God and they to whom the Spirit reveals it; it was something "which none of the princes of the world [that is,
in Paul's time] had known" (1 Corinthians 2:7–9).
Princes then were the choicest men in the world for
natural or acquired parts, but they were ignorant in
this.

2. The other reason why this new way to life is so
commonly missed is from the nature of man; it's a way
that goes against the grain of proud nature. The natural spirit of man makes a stop here as Balaam's ass did
in Numbers 22. There is an innate and hereditary pride
in men to own no other righteousness that would
eclipse theirs. Men are naturally so. Adam's poor con-
trivance to cover his nakedness tells us this. When men
think of going to heaven, they fasten upon something
of their own: "Master, what good thing shall I do?" and
"All these have I kept" (Matthew 19). This man had self-
righteousness at his fingertips, as Paul himself had
while a Pharisee: "As concerning the law, blameless"
(Philippians 3). Self in man is like the heart in man,
which is the last thing to die; it is the fort that holds
out longest against submission to this righteousness of
Christ, like the fort of the Jebusites in 2 Samuel 5 which

would not yield till David stormed it.

Man's good opinion of his own righteousness is among those imaginations or proud reasonings in men that exalt themselves, and are not easily brought under and subdued to the obedience of Christ (2 Corinthians 10:5).

Natural men exalt their own righteousness in opposition to God in various ways:

• It is too usual with some among us to think to recompense God and stop the mouth of His justice by some good works of their own. This popery is in many who would disdain the very name of being a Romanist. Something or other of their own that seems lovely in their eyes, as that Pharisee's fasting did in Luke 18, stands in place of Christ; something of their own doing must do the deed. "Master, what good thing *shall I do* to inherit eternal life?" Here they hang their hopes, and Christ is made merely a useless hanger-on.

• Some make a mixture and composition of their own righteousness and Christ together in their justification, as some of the Galatians did. Some men dare not venture their souls on Christ alone; they'll have two strings to their bow, something of their own at least for a reserve, as those many who believed on Jesus (John 2:23–24): their faith was a halting and divided faith, and therefore He did not commit Himself to them. These men, like the harlot who came to Solomon, would have their living child divided. So many would have their justification before God to be divided between Christ's righteousness and their own.

There are some who, though they do not mix Christ's righteousness and their own, would make theirs a bridge and passage to His. Such are they who would have Christ, but would have Him for their money. Vega said, "I will purchase heaven, not have it as the gift of God." They reject the apostle's doctrine that it is a free gift (Romans 6:23); nor will they buy without money and without price, according to the free invitation given in Isaiah 55:2.

Some goodness of their own must usher them into Christ. They are shy to go to Him only with their sins, their nothingness, and their nakenedness, which men should do. Some men try to be worthy of Christ receiving and owning them. Their theology is like that of the Jews when they urged Christ to go to the centurion's house with this argument: "for he is worthy" (Luke 7:4). These men would commend themselves to Christ by something that is lovely in them; but this is not Christ's way. He did not come to call the righteous, but sinners to repentance; and it is not the well, but the sick who need the Physician. When men are naked, then He casts His skirts over them; and when they are in their blood, this is His time of love, and then He says to them, "Live" (Ezekiel 16).

• There are some men who would think much of it not to be esteemed Christians, and yet look after justification and salvation neither by Christ's righteousness, nor by any of their own, but think that God will forgive and save them in due time without any ado. Any way is the way to heaven, and they think their profaneness will be no more an impediment to heaven than their inheritances on earth. They can be rich and wicked, honorable and wicked, and wise and wicked; and therefore they can be wicked and still go to heaven.

These are the generation of men of whom Moses speaks in Deuteronomy 29:19: "They bless themselves in their heart and say, 'We shall have peace though we walk in the imagination of our hearts and add drunkenness to thirst." They are like desperate riders who leave the highway and venture their bones and necks over hedges and ditches. It is said that eels are bred from putrefaction rather than generation; so this generation of men think to get as near a passage to heaven by profanenness as by holiness. Do not tell them either of imputed righteousness or inherent righteousness; they'll venture their own way. But it is as sure as the Word of God is sure that God will keep these men out of heaven: "There shall by no means enter any that work abominations" (Revelation 21:27); no place but hell is fit for them. The very ox and ass have better names on earth than these have (Isaiah 1).

USE OF EXHORTATION. This doctrine is useful for exhortation to two sorts of men: To those who have not come into this righteousness (Psalm 69:27), as some such there are; and to those who have attained to it and know it, and to those who would know it.

I will address, first, those who have not yet come to seek this righteousness. To them I say two things:

1. Seek this righteousness and none other for your justification; and seek it till you get into such experiential acquaintance with it as to know what you say when you speak of it. Seek the kingdom of God and the righteousness thereof. No other righteousness can expiate your sins but Christ's; nor can any present you without spot to God but His. This is God's righteousness, therefore let it be yours. It is God's because it is a righteousness of God's ordaining, because it is a righteousness of God's imputing, and because it is a righteousness of God's accepting. It is a sufficient righteousness to God and it is a sufficient righteousness to the distressed case of a sinner. Therefore seek this only. Oh, learn to speak the language of Isaiah 45:24–25: "In the Lord have I righteousness. In the Lord shall all the seed of Israel be blessed."

There are many false righteousnesses, as there were many false gods, even in the church of God in the Old Testament, and as there are many false Christs in the New Testament. So take heed of deceiving yourselves, of being deceived with a false righteousness.

Men are exceedingly apt to sit down in a self-righteousness, to warm themselves at the sparks of their own fire. It's as hard to bring men into a better opinion of another's righteousness than of their own, as it was for Elisha to persuade Naaman into higher thoughts of the waters of Jordan, than of Abana and Pharphar in his own country. It's hard for men to count those things which were or are gain to them to be loss for Christ, as Paul did in Philippians 3. Men may be brought to think of themselves as lost for their sins, but hardly for their righteousness.

And therefore, the Holy Ghost tells us that it is the exceeding greatness of God's power, even the working of His mighty power—that power that raised Christ from the dead when such a weight as the sins of the world and the curse of the law was upon Him—to keep Him under the power of death. Yea, the Spirit of God says that it is such a power, and nothing less, that must make a sinner to believe in Christ for righteousness and life.

How many set their tears, sighs, and groans for sin in Christ's place, and in place of His righteousness? How many set their desires of grace, their much praying and hearing, and their dislike of evil ways in the place of this righteousness? They do it, but they do not think that they do it. The Assyrian had this commission and charge from the Lord, to make the great spoils he did. "Howbeit he meaneth not so, neither doth his heart think so" (Isaiah 10:5–7).

Indeed, these above-mentioned good and holy things, such as sighs for sin and desires for grace, are signs that follow them who believe in Christ for righteousness, but they are not the grounds of a man's expecting righteousness by Christ. There must be your own nothingness and a lost condition in yourself, and then God's free grace and Jesus Christ in a free promise.

The justifying act of faith is laid on such ground work as this: A man must be convinced of sin and of his own unrighteousness. Now is the season for him to cast himself on Christ's righteousness as it is freely offered him by God in His gospel, just as the season for diseased people to go into the pool for healing was when the angel moved the water (John 5). So it is the proper season to fly to Christ for sanctuary when a sinner sees himself undone in and by himself. This is the justifying act of faith.

Men have reason to suspect their faith that is drawn out to Christ because of some self-worth; for true, saving faith has no footing to stand on but free grace and the free gift of Christ. And look to it, for all other faith in Christ will fail you when it comes to a pinch, and when conscience indeed lacks satisfaction. The greater confidence men have by a false or, though true, an insufficient faith, the greater will be their despair when the fallacy is seen. Oh, take heed of this fallacy; beware of embracing bleary-eyed Leah for beautiful Rachel!

It's a dangerous thing to set up our own righteousness, graces, duties, and works as qualifications for our faith in Christ; this is but clear poison. As God hangs the earth upon nothing, so must we hang the righteousness of Christ upon our own nothingness. Grace and good works are not the way to our justification by Christ, though they are the way to heaven.

I cannot easily exceed in caution in this case. Men may make other things besides Christ their righteousness interpretatively on God's part when they do not do it intentionally on their own. A man who is eager for riches or honor does not think that he makes these things his god; it is not his intention, and yet it is in God's account, who calls covetousness "idolatry." And many make their belly their god who do not think so. So we may not intend to make anything our righteousness but Christ, and yet may warp in practice. A man may be an atheist in practice who is not so in judgment, and so may be a self-righteous man. Therefore, let us take heed to our spirits in this point.

2. Seek this righteousness of Christ in God's way of giving it, that is, by imputation. He imputes it to him who believes in Jesus, not to him who works: "To him that worketh not, but believeth on Him that justifies the ungodly, his faith is counted by God for righteousness."

We must look after this righteousness of Christ to be made ours as it is offered of free grace and in a free promise. Is it not a strange thing that a man should more easily believe in Christ when he can see some good in himself than when he can see nothing but Christ in a free promise? Yet it is so: as if something in himself were better footing for faith in Christ than God's free grace and the free offer of Christ and His righteousness to him as a lost sinner.

Oh, how this self sticks to a man! But certainly, the less we see in ourselves, the more inducement it should be to cast ourselves on Jesus Christ. For what is it that can answer the law, our own accusing, troubled conscience, or the devil's charge against us, but the righteousness of Christ made ours by free grace? It was Christ who took Satan's charge against Joshua, the Jews' high priest (Zechariah 3:2). And Jesus Christ the righteous is our advocate with the Father (1 John 2:1).

The righteousness of Christ is fitted to the sinner's condition; it's open to Adam and his seed as fallen, not as standing. The serpent was for the Israelites who were stung, not for those who were whole. A sinner must take this righteousness as a sinner, let his sins be as the sands or stars, as crimson or scarlet. Christ's righteousness is fitted for such sinners when convinced and humbled, for that woman in Luke 7 who had no other name given her but that of a sinner.

The brazen serpent was not lifted up because of gnats, but because of the stinging of fiery serpents. And Christ came to save not only the least of sinners, but the chief of sinners. Christ brought no petty cures, but such as physicians could not do, as we see in the case of the woman with the issue of blood and the man's son whom the disciples could not cure (Matthew 9 and 17). Where sin abounds, Christ's righteousness is ordained to superabound. The way is opened to Christ for all sinners who come weary and burdened to Him. He bids none of them stand back. "Him that cometh to Me I will in no wise cast out" (John 6:37). There is more danger of their missing this righteousness who have something of their own to trust in than of theirs who have nothing. Christ sends the rich away empty. Fewer scribes and Pharisees believed on Christ than publicans and sinners (Luke 1).

Remember, then, that this is the righteousness which ends all controversy between God and a sinner, and between the law and a sinner, and which also ends all quarrels in a poor sinner's conscience. God says that He is satisfied with this righteousness: "The Lord is well-pleased for His righteousness' sake" (Isaiah 42: 21). The law is satisfied with this righteousness: "Christ is the end of the law for righteousness to everyone that believeth" (Romans 10:4). And conscience says, "I am satisfied with this righteousness." "Being justified by faith, we have peace with God through our Lord Jesus Christ" (Romans 5:1).

A sleepy conscience may be satisfied with self-righteousness, but an awakened conscience cannot be. Therefore, seek this righteousness of Christ, and seek it only, in the case of justification; and seek it in God's way of giving it, the way of imputation, in the way of free grace, and in a free promise, without respect to anything in yourselves. "We are justified freely by His grace through the redemption that is in Christ Jesus" (Romans 3:24).

Second, I will address this exhortation to such as have made the righteousness of Christ theirs, and who know it, or who would know it. To such I say these things:

Be sure to keep a distinction between Christ's imputed righteousness and your own inherent righteousness when you think of your discharge from sin and being righteous before God. Remember that Jacob put on his elder brother's garments when he went to his father for the blessing. And let me tell you that for a man to depend on his own righteousness is a greater sin than his unrighteousness; for this is a sin against the law, and that is a sin against the gospel. It is true, a godly man ought to approve himself to God in the sincerity of his inherent grace and righteousness, and take much comfort when he can do so. Thus did Paul: "This is our rejoicing, the testimony of our conscience, that in simplicity and godly sincerity we have had our conversation in this world" (2 Corinthians 1:12); and he advised Timothy to study to approve himself to God. Enoch had this testimony, that he pleased God in his walking.

But though we please God as our Father with our graces and the sincerity of our lives, yet we cannot satisfy His justice as a Judge with these; we cannot bring these to God in the point of our justification. Joseph said to his brothers, "Bring Benjamin, or else ye cannot see my face" (Genesis 43). So it is with us: if we do not bring Christ and His righteousness made ours to God, we cannot see His face.

God stands on it that we expect justification merely

by His grace and not by our own. In Naaman's free cure of his leprosy, he would have given the prophet gifts for his cure. But the prophet said, "As the Lord liveth, before whom I stand, I shall receive none" (2 Kings 5:16). Men should therefore shun that patched righteousness and way of justification invented by the false apostles in the holy apostles' days, as we see in Paul's epistles to the Romans and the Galatians. The Jews trusted their own righteousness, and many mongrel Christians mixed Christ's and their own; they jumbled the two covenants together, half Christ and half works, in the point of a sinner's justification. They were like those children of the Jews (Nehemiah 13:24) who married wives of Ashdod: they spoke half in the language of Ashdod and half in the language of the Jews. And thus do they of the church of Rome, though many of them can speak a purer gospel when they come to die.

We find in the Levitical law that God would have no honey used in sacrifice to Him (Leviticus 2:11); for though it is sweet, yet it breeds choler in the stomach. Thus God will have man's righteousness to have nothing to do in his justification, because, though it is sweet and pleasant in its place, yet here it would swell and puff up.

That was a brave speech of Luther's on Galatians, being rightly interpreted: "Let Moses be dead and buried, and his sepulcher never be found." I take his meaning to be the exclusion of the works of Moses' law from a man's justification, and from being his righteousness before God. This would be in accordance with Acts 13:39: "And by Him all that believe are justified from all things, from which he could not be justified by the law of Moses." But whether God hinted at this to us in burying Moses' body Himself and concealing the place of his burial, I do not know.

Yet we must still be urged to keep a distinction between Christ's righteousness and our own, so as to see a need of His when our own is nearest to perfection, and to see His as necessary when we are at the acme of grace, as when we first came out of our natural state. For surely we may expect that when we come to die we shall find we must have a stronger supporter for our hearts and hopes than our inherent righteousness. If then we will ease our troubled minds, we must lean and lay our weight on the free grace of God in Christ.

Truly, this is the way to avoid both rocks and sand, to escape the snare that is in our most perfect graces and duties, and also to have comfort in our weakest ones. Our completed graces will not infect us with pride and exalt us above measure, nor will our lowest measures perplex us. For now, when we see ourselves as wretched in ourselves, as Paul did, then we can say with him that we thank God for Jesus Christ, and take sanctuary there.

I close this branch of exhortation with the words of David and Isaiah as well-becoming us: "I will make mention of Thy righteousness, of Thine only" (Psalm 71:16). And "Surely one shall say, In the Lord have I righteousness; in the Lord shall all the seed of Israel be justified" (Isaiah 45:24–25).

Now, let Christians who have attained to this righteousness learn how to raise and extract strong consolation from it, and to take this as a cordial in the droopings of their souls by the remainders of sin: "Christ is the Lord Our Righteousness."

Who among the saints of God on earth have not experienced, more or less, what trouble of conscience is, and how weak a cordial the best of their own is to their hearts at such a season. This made blessed Paul say, "Not mine own righteousness, but that of God by faith in Christ." This will raise up the most sinking spirits, and those consciences that are most in despair. It's by this righteousness that God justifies the ungodly.

And God expresses two reasons why He justifies man by this righteousness: To exclude boasting, and to prevent terrors of conscience in His people from their common sense of little grace and much sin in themselves.

It is this righteousness that is the foundation of peace with God and of peace in our own conscience. The terrors of conscience for sin are removed and abolished by the coming in of this righteousness when applied and improved.

It's true that the sanctification of our natures and the holiness of our lives are a good secondary supporter of peace in our consciences: "This is our rejoicing, the testimony of our consciences, that in simplicity and godly sincerity, not in fleshly wisdom, but by the grace of God, we have had our conversation in this world." The saints' own righteousnesses and graces do not have that sovereign power to pacify the disturbed conscience, as the righteousness of Christ has.

Saul had many worthy men in his army, but only David could encounter Goliath. So there is worth and excellency in the inherent graces of believers, and in their personal righteousness, but it is this imputed righteousness alone that can encounter the charge of the law, of Satan, and of our own consciences.

And truly this righteousness of Christ imputed to a believer and applied by him makes his conscience like the land of Canaan, a place of sweet rest and repose, "the rest of God," as it is called. Now there is nothing but amicable carriage between God and the soul. When Abraham was righteous by believing the promised seed, then he was called "the friend of God" (James 2:23). Yea, he was His bosom friend: "Shall I hide from Abraham the thing that I shall do?" (Genesis 18:17). Indeed the very scope of this imputed righteousness is to remove all difference between God and us.

It is true, there is *amor beneplaciti,* a love of goodwill, which God bore to us before our justification, when we were in our blood (Ezekiel 16:6). But His love of complacency and delight does not appear till we have this righteousness on us; then it is that we are beautiful in His eyes, even through His comeliness put upon us. Now it is that Christ speaks such language to His spouse: "Behold, thou art fair, My love, behold, thou art fair. Thou hast ravished My heart, My sister, My spouse; thou hast ravished My heart with one of thine eyes" (Song of Solomon 4:1, 9).

It is now that there is nearness to God. We are "a people near unto Him" (Psalm 148:14). Now there is that mysterious oneness between the Father, Christ, and believers: "In that day ye shall know that I am in My Father, and you in Me, and I in you" (John 14:20). Now there may be as blessed interview between these three as was between the angel and Jacob, between the Lord and Moses, and as will be between God and the children of Israel in the latter days mentioned in Hosea 3:3: "I will be for thee, and thou shalt be for Me." Now there may be the enjoyment of that communion and fellowship with the Father and His Son Jesus Christ that fills the heart with joy. And now a man may have that boldness and liberty with God "in whom we have boldness and access with confidence by the faith of Him" (Ephesians 3:12).

Remember then that this righteousness of Christ imputed to a humble sinner is a cure for all extremities of conscience. When a poor souls says to itself, "Shall such a wretch as I be justified before God?" The answer should be, "Why, why *not* I?" By this righteousness God justifies the ungodly, that is, objectively, when they are such, though they are not such after they are justified.

Here's the magazine of comfort for all believers:

The weak believer has the same beauty and loveliness in him, in God's eyes, by this righteousness as the strongest, John's "little children" every bit as much as his "young men" and "fathers." And once a man has attained to this righteousness, it does not matter whether he was a lesser or a greater sinner before; for however great a sinner has been before he believed in Christ for this righteousness of his, yet now that he does believe, all his sins and unrighteousness are swallowed up into victory by it, even though, he had been the chief of sinners, which was Paul's case.

Now there are two things in this imputed righteousness which make it the spring of such strong consolation:

1. It is everlasting righteousness (Daniel 9:24), and so is a covering for sins to come as well as sins past; therefore it is set out by a fountain (Zechariah 13:1). Adam's righteousness in his state of innocence, and that of the angels too, was but a cistern, apt to dry up; but Christ's is a fountain-righteousness, and so an everlasting righteousness, to make an end of sin, to make reconciliation for iniquity, and to bring in everlasting righteousness, as Daniel says.

It was a great miracle which the Lord did for the children of Israel in the wilderness, when their clothes did not wax old in forty years time. But that was nothing compared to this everlasting righteousness which God imputes to believers; this will never wax old. The heavens will wax old (Psalm 102:26), but this righteousness is as fresh as ever, and so will be forever: "Thy righteousness is an everlasting righteousness" (Psalm 119:142). Though Christ was but once offered on earth, yet He is a continual, sweet odor offered to God for us in heaven.

2. It is infinite righteousness, and this suits the sinner's state, who needs infinite righteousness. The

greatest sinner needs no more than this righteousness to justify him in the sight of God; and the least sinner needs as much. Just so, he who gathered much manna had nothing left over, and he who gathered little had no lack (Exodus 16:18). The least sin is unpardonable without this righteousness, and the greatest sins are pardonable by it, except the sin against the Holy Ghost.

Indeed, to think any sin is little is a great sin, because the least sin must have this righteousness, this everlasting and infinite righteousness, for a covering. And yet for a man not to believe Christ's righteousness is above all sin is a greater sin; for disobedience is the disobedience of man, but the obedience of Christ is the obedience of God-man. The sin of man is infinite only improperly, that is, in respect of the object against whom it is committed, God; but the obedience and righteousness of Christ is properly infinite in respect of its Subject, by whom it was acted, He who was God as well as man. The transgressor of the law was but man, but the Satisfier of the law was God also. And hereupon we are to make these three observations:

OBSERVATION 1. See the great honor done to the law by this righteousness, that the law should be so abundantly satisfied by the righteousness of such a person as the Lord Jesus Christ.

OBSERVATION 2. See the great security of the humbled and believing sinner, who has such righteousness and obedience made over to him as the righteousness of God; for so this righteousness of Christ is often called, and so it is indeed.

OBSERVATION 3. See how God, Christ, the believer, and the gospel, as well as the law, all gain by this way of a sinner being made righteous.

As for God, it is to the praise of the glory of His grace, wherein "we are accepted in the Beloved" (Ephesians 1:6).

As for Christ, He is on this account highly exalted, even in His human nature (Philippians 2:8–9).

As for the gospel, it is hereby made a glorious gospel, the ministration of the Spirit, and the ministration of righteousness which exceeds in glory.

As for the believer, his condition and his comfort are wonderfully secured, as well as his honor in this point, above the angels, to whom Christ is not made righteousness, like His is to men who believe. Christ did not take on Himself the nature of angels (Hebrews 2:16), but the seed of Abraham. So He does not put His righteousness on the angels, but on the spiritual seed of Abraham. These are they who have white robes, which is "the righteousness of the saints" (Revelation 19:8).

Consider further that the righteousness of Christ not only covers the sins of believers, but their righteousness too, that is, the imperfections of their graces, duties, and works, and procures for them acceptance with God. It does for them what the sweet frankincense in the law (Leviticus 2) did for the sacrifices then, make them a sweet savor to Jehovah.

We have cause indeed to mourn over our holy duties and best works, as in themselves and as being from us; yet we have reason to rejoice in them as veiled with this righteousness, which is for our duties as well as our persons. This was shadowed by the plate of pure gold (Exodus 28:36), having engraven on it, "Holiness to the Lord," and put on the forehead of Aaron that he might bear the iniquity of the holy things of the children of Israel, and that they might be accepted before the Lord. That was the antitype of this, as the apostle shows in Hebrews 13:20–21: "Now the God of peace that brought again from the dead our Lord Jesus, that great Shepherd of the sheep, through the blood of the everlasting covenant, make you perfect in every good work to do

His will, working in you that which is well-pleasing in His sight, through Jesus Christ."

It is by this righteousness that the duties, works, and graces of believers shall appear to honor, praise, and glory at the appearing of Jesus Christ. And, upon the account of this imputed righteousness, the obedience of one believer is more acceptable with God than the obedience of all mankind in the first covenant.

Oh, the wonderful satisfaction which a believer may take in this righteousness. God does so: "The Lord is well-pleased for His righteousness sake" (Isaiah 42:21). And well may we then. But how few do! Some of these few do not because they cannot; though they have attained to this righteousness, yet they have not attained to the sense of it. All believers have the same state of peace because they are in the same state of justification, but they do not all have the same sense of peace. Though there is the same reason for it in respect of this righteousness, for it is a covering to the weakest believer as well as the strongest, yet all do not have the assuring act of faith. There may be faith where there is not sight. "Faith is the evidence of things not seen" or felt (Hebrews 11:1; 2 Corinthians 5:7).

And the reason for this uncertainty in some of God's people is their listening to unjust judges. Satan is a malicious judge, and he has influence sometimes upon poor souls to dazzle their evidence. Carnal reasoning, self-imagination, and pre-suppositions are erroneous judges also.

Your appeals, therefore, must be to God in your case: "I will hearken what the Lord God shall speak" (Psalm 85:8). The Spirit must convince men of righteousness as well as of sin. It is not easy for a godly man to take in the comfort of a justified state. Presumptuous men indeed take comfort easily; they catch it before their time. They are like Saul, who would sacrifice before Samuel came, contrary to order. These are as bold in their claim of what is not yet theirs as the harlot was of the living child in 1 Kings 3. But true believers come by their comfort and assurance with difficulty, as that chief captain did by his Roman freedom (Acts 22:28).

These are sometimes in Job's dissatisfaction, when he said, "If I had called and He had answered me, yet would I not believe that He had hearkened to my voice" (Job 9:16). Though Nathan told David that the Lord had put away his sin (2 Samuel 12:13), yet David did not feel the comfort of it; and therefore how he prayed and cried for pardon, and for the restoring of the joy of God's salvation (Psalm 51)!

God will have His people know that not only justification, but the comfort of a justified state, is the free gift of God.

QUESTION. How may the evidence of the righteousness of Christ made ours be come by?

ANSWER 1. By the conviction of the Spirit. And there is a twofold conviction of the Spirit in this case: First, that Christ has such a righteousness for sinners, which He proves in this way: Christ has gone to the Father, and this righteousness is imputed to us who believe. Though it is there written, yet the Spirit must convince us of it by a reflex act of faith; and the Spirit has such an office: "He shall receive of Mine, and shall show it unto you" (John 16:14). "We have received the Spirit which is of God that we might know the things that are freely given us of God" (1 Corinthians 2:12).

And this the Spirit does in giving us the reflex act of faith, which is the assurance of faith. 2 Timothy 1:12: "I know whom I have believed." 1 John 5:20: "And hath given us an understanding to know Him, and that we are in Him." Thus the Spirit puts to silence all anxious disputes in the case. Oh, pray and wait for this conviction of the Spirit if you do not yet have it!

ANSWER 2. The exercise of faith is necessary to our having evidence of this righteousness being ours. Faith is of necessary use to make it ours, and the exercise of faith is of necessary use to discover it to be ours. The use of faith is not only to bring us into a justified state, but also to give us the evidence and comfort of that state, which it must do by its being exercised. Romans 1:17: "The righteousness of God is revealed from faith to faith." Justification requires faith, and the assurance of it requires faith upon faith, which gives the full assurance of it (Hebrews 10:22).

Surely it is to be lamented that ancient and experienced Christians, who perhaps have been long in the possession of their justification, are yet often questioning their title; this is by remitting the acts of faith. Christ did not do much for men and places where He did not find faith. He gave His disciples this reason why they could not heal the man's child: "because of their unbelief." Their faith was too low. And His words to them may be often applied to us: "Oh, fools, and slow of heart to believe" (Luke 24:25).

Therefore, when we fathom the depth of our being made righteous by the righteousness of Christ made ours, and find our evidence shallow, as they found the sea to be in Acts 27, we must do as they did: cast anchor, and set faith hard at work on this righteousness of Christ offered to a believer sinner in a free promise.

QUESTION. But how may I know that I have this righteousness?

ANSWER. Why, consider the concomitants and consequences of it; and if you have these, you have that.

First, this righteousness will ever throw down self-righteousness. Where this righteousness has not been attained, there self-righteousness is set up; and where it is, self-righteousness is cast down. Persons justified by free grace lie low in themselves. Poverty of spiritual and habitual self-abasement are very discernible in them.

Second, imputed righteousness is ever accompanied with inherent righteousness in its capable subjects. Romans 8:4: "That the righteousness of the law may be fulfilled in us who walk not after the flesh, but after the Spirit." And 1 John 3:7: "He that doth righteousness is righteous, even as He is." There is no such friend to holiness as this righteousness of free grace. Where was there a more holy man in his day than Paul, who was so experimentally versed in the imputed righteousness of Christ? Inherent holiness faces imputed righteousness and receives life from it, as the moon receives light from the sun.

It is evident in the Holy Scriptures that the faith that justifies makes pure work in men who have it. Acts 15:9: "Purifying their hearts by faith." Peter calls it "precious faith" in 2 Peter 1:1. It makes precious works where it is; and what precious work is there in a loose, carnal, drunken, worldly, merely formal believer? Where this precious faith is, there will be precious things: a precious heart, a precious life, precious duties, a precious conduct, precious experiences, and precious enjoyments.

And truly, faith separated from these is but a ghost of faith, like Saul's fulfilling the commandment of the Lord though he had spared Agag and the fat of the cattle. Loose believers bring an ill report on this doctrine of imputed righteousness, like the spies did of the land of Canaan; they make it to have ill favor with anti-Christian unbelievers, like Simeon and Levi did their father and his family among the inhabitants of the land, and as the wickedness of the sons of Eli made the offering of the Lord to be abhorred by the people (Genesis 34:30; 1 Samuel 2:17).

James 2, and other parallel passages in the Word of God, may grip the consciences of such believers whose faith is without works, unless they are dead works and works of darkness, and unless their consciences are dead as well. Faith and good works are like Saul and Jonathan, lovely and not divided, as David said of them. Therefore those Christians who divide justifying faith and holiness of life do as Jereboam did in dividing the ten tribes from the two. Christ's righteousness on us has a righteousness in us, wrought by His Spirit to attend it.

This righteousness of Christ imputed to men is like that tree of life (Revelation 22:2) which bore various manners of fruit, and that every month, and whose leaves were for the healing of the nations. This tree of life is the Lord Jesus Christ, who, by His merit and Spirit, converts heathens into saints, and makes saints bring forth the saving fruits of righteousness. Philippians 1:11: "Being filled with the fruits of righteousness, which are by Jesus Christ, which are unto the glory and praise of God." The woman who is joined to a man is one flesh, and the man who is joined to Christ is one spirit. The same mind is in him which was in Christ Jesus, and he is, in his desire and endeavor, of the same manner of life, which is for obedience to the will of God.

USE OF INSTRUCTION. Let this new and strange way of God's justifying us, even when we were ungodly, teach and move us to justify God in the strangest of His providences to ourselves or towards His church. Christ justified us when we were at our worst; and why, then, should we not justify the worst of Christ, even His cross and sufferings from offense and scandal? His righteousness makes our persons and performances, though full of imperfections, sweet and lovely to God. And let the thought of this make our sufferings for Him, with all their bitterness, lovely to us. They were so to blessed Paul: "I take pleasure in infirmities, in re-